Splitsville

Splitsville

HOW TO SEPARATE,
STAY OUT OF COURT
AND STAY FRIENDS

Clarissa Rayward

GRAMMAR
FACTORY
— EST^D 2013 —

Splitsville, Second Edition

Published by Grammar Factory Publishing, an imprint of MacMillan Company Limited.

Grammar Factory Publishing
MacMillan Company Limited
25 Telegram Mews, 39th Floor, Suite 3906
Toronto, Ontario, Canada
M5V 3Z1

www.grammarfactory.com

Rayward, Clarissa.
Splitsville: How to Separate, Stay Out of Court and Stay Friends / Clarissa Rayward.

Paperback ISBN 978-0-9942025-0-5
eBook ISBN 978-0-9942025-1-2
Audiobook ISBN 978-1-996867-04-4

1. FAM015000 FAMILY & RELATIONSHIPS / Divorce & Separation.
2. LAW038020 LAW / Family Law / Divorce & Separation.
3. FAM013000 FAMILY & RELATIONSHIPS / Conflict Resolution.

Production Credits
Cover design by Lauren Jenning
Book production and editorial services by Grammar Factory Publishing

Grammar Factory's Carbon Neutral Publishing Commitment
Grammar Factory Publishing is proud to be neutralising the carbon footprint of all printed copies of its authors' books printed by or ordered directly through Grammar Factory or its affiliated companies through the purchase of Gold Standard-Certified International Offsets.

Contents

INTRODUCTION

The 'D' Word

Sometimes
good things
fall apart so
better things
can fall together.

MARILYN MONROE

The 'D' Word

We often joke about the 'D' word (divorce), but for those of us who are experiencing or have experienced the breakdown of a significant relationship it is anything but a humorous experience. In divorce, there are no winners. A successful divorce, if ever there was such a thing, is not about winning battles but instead about resolving differences.

Unfortunately, many don't see it that way and, having had the privilege of practising in Family Law for over twenty-five years with over 5,000 families, I have seen firsthand the damage that can be done to parents, children, families and friends as a result of an adversarial legal process.

Divorce is said to be one of the most significant grief events many of us will ever suffer. Is it any wonder then that, during divorce, good people suddenly seem to be mad?

As a Divorce Lawyer I have seen it all. People who in any other situation are entirely 'normal' suddenly turn into crazy versions of themselves – acting in ways even they would never expect. You see, heartbreak does this to us. Love is a roller coaster of exhilarating highs and sometimes the lowest of lows. Perhaps the lowest moment for many of us is that moment when you realise that love has passed, that moment when your stomach has that sick, sinking feeling and you realise love, as you wanted it, is over.

If falling in love is a romance novel, then heartbreak would have to be a choose your own adventure book – while it seems like you should have control, you don't and it feels like you are turning pages of your life hoping the ending will be good, only to have to turn back four chapters and start all over again. Like any good novel though, it does come to an end – eventually.

Just like falling in love, we all experience heartbreak in our own way. For some of us, it might appear to the outside world to have had no impact at all, but that person's insides will be tearing apart as they try to manage their grief. Others will run around the streets screaming at the top of their lungs, letting everyone know their pain. And most of us will fall somewhere between these two extremes.

Relationships encompass so much of our lives and yet we are given so little education in how to fall in love, stay in love and fall out of love. Divorce is still such a 'dirty' word, and yet if you choose to get married there is a 50/50 chance that divorce will form part of your marriage. So why is it that divorce continues to be such a dirty word? Why is it that we can't start to see a divorce as part of a marriage – the part where you could constructively say 'thank you' for the experiences and time you have shared together?

I believe it is time that we rethink the word 'divorce'. It should not be a scary word, a dirty word or something we are embarrassed by. A divorce should be seen as a part of a marriage that, when managed well, we can look back on with some pride.

Several years ago, Gwyneth Paltrow and Chris Martin captured public attention when they described their separation as 'conscious uncoupling'. Rather than framing their decision as a divorce, they spoke about making a conscious choice to end their marriage respectfully. While the term itself attracted plenty of commentary, what stood out was the idea that separation could be approached intentionally – and differently.

It can be done. But it requires a choice. And ideally, it is a choice made together.

That doesn't mean that your heart won't still break, that you won't want to yell and scream. But the choice you are making is that no matter what, you will try, together, to find a way to consciously fall out of love with respect, dignity and even some grace.

In writing this book I have spent countless hours rethinking 'divorce'. When the Family Law Act (Cth) came into effect here in Australia in 1975, getting a divorce was a very different thing from what it is now. Now divorce is commonplace – certainly not easy, but more accepted by society than ever before. For this reason, I believe it is time we started to change how we think about divorce and that people like me, family lawyers and all of us in the Family Law system, focus on ensuring that couples are able to bring an end to their relationships with dignity and grace.

This is the second edition of *Splitsville*, written more than a decade after the first. In that time, there have been significant changes in Australian Family Law, making this update necessary to ensure the information you are reading is current and accurate (before it all changes again!).

One big change is the approach and understanding of some of the most difficult dynamics that exist in so many relationships – family violence, addiction, drug and alcohol misuse and many other challenging behaviours that create significant challenges for families. When I first wrote *Splitsville*, I was careful to acknowledge that the idea of being 'friends' with someone who has caused you harm is often not necessary or realistic and so I would say, 'This book probably isn't for you,' if you are managing these difficult dynamics in your relationship.

A decade on, my thinking has evolved. These issues are far more prevalent than we once acknowledged, and as a society and within the legal system we are better equipped to identify, understand and respond to risk. I have seen meaningful shifts in how the system recognises and manages the impact of family violence and other serious challenges on parents and children.

So sure, the idea of being 'friends' doesn't need to be on your wish list, but whatever has occurred in your relationship, I would still say that the information, approach and framework in *Splitsville* can still help empower you to make informed decisions that prioritise safety, dignity and long-term wellbeing for yourself and your family.

If you are reading this book and are worried for your or someone else's safety, always call **Triple Zero (000)** if there is immediate danger. For non-emergency support, I always recommend **1800RESPECT (1800 737 732)** for counselling and safety planning.

A successful divorce,

if ever there was such a thing,

is not about

winning battles

but instead about

resolving differences.

ANNE'S STORY

A few years ago, I had the opportunity to assist Anne, a thirty-five-year-old woman who had found herself stuck in the Family Court system. She was facing an application relating to the time her three-year-old son James would spend with his father, Bill.

Anne had fallen pregnant with James unexpectedly after having a fleeting relationship with Bill. Only a few months into her pregnancy, Anne found herself seeking legal advice as she and Bill could not communicate even on the simplest level. Bill refused to communicate with Anne and Anne thought there was no other way than to engage a solicitor to communicate with Bill on her behalf.

Anne was a well-educated professional from a caring family. She had not envisaged that she would find herself in the circumstances that she did.

Picture yourself, an expectant parent, not able to even pick up the phone to the mother or father of your unborn child and discuss what for most of us is the most exciting thing that will happen in our lives. Imagine instead that you are spending thousands of dollars corresponding through lawyers in letters with the mother or father of your child.

I remember well those nine (almost ten) long months that I carried my first daughter. It was a tumultuous time. Alongside the expectation and excitement was much fear and illness. While my husband and I tried to ensure we had everything well organised, I can say it was still a very daunting and grounding experience when we first brought our daughter home. I cannot imagine having to prepare for that day without the support of my husband. I particularly cannot imagine the impact it would have had on me, and no doubt my daughter, had I spent those ten months negotiating with my husband through legal representatives as Anne had done.

Anne had also had a difficult pregnancy with some health scares along the way. Rather than being able to share these challenges with Bill and seek his input and comfort, letters were again exchanged with Bill's lawyers to seek information that any other parents would have been able to share openly and easily over a cup of tea. There was no love. There was no support. There was no communication.

Before James had even been born he was being damaged by parents who had engaged in a legal process that was designed to pit them as adversaries rather than as parents. By the time I met Anne she had spent well over $150,000 in legal fees pursuing a dispute that no longer seemed to have any clarity as to its bounds. James was then three years old.

Anne had not been able to return to her professional career as the legal process had enveloped her life. Between parenting a young boy, reading legal documents and meeting with lawyers, she could not even contemplate where she might be in a few weeks' time, let alone see a light at the end of her tunnel.

And then there was James. Poor James knew nothing other than two parents who, while they loved him, could not even mutter a simple kind word to each other. The first three years of James' life arrived one morning in my office – two large archive boxes full to the brim with paper. Legal letters and documents that sometimes referred to James but seemed to more often refer to Anne and Bill and their distrust of each other. By this stage, Anne and Bill could have purchased a small house for the sum they had invested in the reams of paper in those archive boxes.

Each weekend, James went from Anne to Bill and back again on the side of a busy road where he cried and cried as he clung to Anne. It was not that James did not enjoy his time with Bill, it was that James knew nothing other than parents who could not even look at each other and say a simple hello. His mother arrived in fear, his father arrived in stoic anger, and James was left to navigate the tricky minefield that is moving between two parents who cannot find a way to put their son's needs above their own.

James would be a teenager now and I don't know what the future holds for him. I do know that his parents will never be able to sit at a table and share a dinner and a conversation with him about his successes at school. I know that when he comes to consider marriage himself, he will sit quietly for some time contemplating which of his parents he might invite to his wedding, as I doubt they could both be there together.

I know he will never look out into the audience of his school auditorium and see both his parents smiling back, sharing in his successes. And I know that James will, at some time in his life, ask himself what he did wrong that his parents can't just sit down together for him.

James will never see the archive boxes of paper that his parents invested every last dollar in, but instead he will see something far more damaging. He will see every other week of his life the two people he loves most in this world hurting each other with their silence.

It is our primary job as parents to raise our children to feel cherished and to enable them to be the very best that they can be and to live a fulfilled life. Anne and Bill in their own ways will tell you that they have raised James so that he feels 'cherished'. They have showered him with gifts, have plans for a good education and provide him with a caring home. And yet, I imagine that when James is old enough to tell us, he will say that he feels anything but cherished.

I worked with Anne for well over a year and saw her through to the 'end' of her legal process. I saw firsthand the damage, despair and emotional upheaval she felt as she found herself before the Family Courts. I also imagine that Bill suffered in a very similar way. And I know that James has already suffered more emotional turmoil than any young man needs.

This is why I know I would do everything I could to ensure my family did not venture into the Family Courts if I experienced a breakdown in my marriage. The Court process, as far as I can tell, has only one advantage: a Court, or a Judge, will ultimately make a decision. They will tell you and your former partner how much time you can spend with your children or how much of your personal wealth and income you can retain.

If you find yourself in the Family Court process, you are in essence 'buying' a decision maker. A person, who knows very little about you and almost nothing about your values or goals in life, who will ultimately tell you how much time you will spend with your children and how much of your hard-earned money you can retain.

Most people that I meet in my role as a family lawyer are more than capable of making decisions that relate to their children and their money – in fact, they do it every day. It seems, however, that the breakdown of a relationship suddenly makes these sorts of decisions very difficult for some people.

In Anne and Bill's case, it was not Anne's fault. Nor was it Bill's. It certainly wasn't James'. In fact, I am not sure we can blame any one person for the difficult mess this family found themselves in.

I am quite sure that if they had their time again, they would both have done something differently. I imagine it would be something as simple as sitting down to have a chat.

Anne and Bill could live their separate lives, they could even choose to not much like each other, but at the end of the day had they just been able to sit down and have an honest conversation it is likely they would never have found themselves where they did some four years later.

Anne and Bill stand out in my mind as a family that really could have found a better way. I have had the joy of working with many families in my time as a family lawyer. I have watched some families negotiate their divorce with respect for each other that is boundless. For others, like James' family, the legal separation process leaves a mark on their lives that will never be forgotten.

It is my observations of families just like Anne's that have led me to want to share with you my knowledge of how you can protect yourself and your family during divorce and separation. There simply is a 'better' and easier way.

There simply
is a **better**
and easier way.

THE LIGHT AT THE END OF THE TUNNEL

One third to one half of all marriages in Australia will end in divorce. Importantly, these statistics do not encompass the increasingly popular de facto relationships - in which people in committed long-term relationships choose not to get married - which have a higher chance of ending in separation than marriages.

In the end, this means that every thirty minutes an Australian child, just like James, will experience family breakdown. For some children, like James, their parents never had any significant relationship to begin with. Regardless, Australian studies have shown that children who experience the separation of their parents are at risk of poorer outcomes in adult life than their peers who have not experienced a family breakdown.

This is the most concerning part of any divorce or separation. While we are very lucky in Australia to have a fair and open Family Court system with committed, intelligent and diligent lawyers and Judges who assist families at very difficult times, your children are still at risk of poorer outcomes in adult life than their peers who do not experience the divorce of their parents.

However, it is important to remember that it is not your divorce that can cause harm to your children; it is the conflict that often ensues long after your separation that is the cause of harm. When children experience the two most important people in their lives in conflict day in and day out, those children are deeply affected and cannot go on to achieve their full potential.

So what do we do? I am not suggesting that you should not divorce, as research tells us that unhappy relationships also take their toll on our children. However, there are many 'better' options than the Court process for separating families to resolve legal differences. This book will show you how.

Splitsville will guide you through the legal separation and divorce process in the least damaging way for both you and your family so that you can experience a dignified divorce.

While this book will guide you through the legal issues that may flow from the end of your marriage or de facto relationship, there will be many other issues that you will have to navigate as you move through your separation. In *Part 1 – Where do I start?* I'll share with you the exercise I give all my clients who are contemplating whether separation is the right choice, as well as some strategies to manage your grief and start your separation on the right foot. How you behave in the very early stages of your separation will have a significant impact on the resolution of any legal issues, how quickly (or slowly) you might get there, and your future relationship with your former spouse, so I urge you to take the time to read this part of the book before moving on.

Part 2 will cover the three main legal issues that arise in a separation – parenting arrangements, the division of your financial affairs and, if you are married, the dissolution of your marriage – and the law's stance on each of these.

Part 3 – The legal process will show you the range of options you have for finalising the legal aspects of your separation, including options outside the Family Court process. Here I'll also cover how to amicably negotiate with your spouse, a range of advisers who may be able to assist, and the paperwork you'll need to finalise the legal matters relating to your separation.

Finally, *Part 4 – Moving* on will cover your life after your separation, including some tips to help you move forward and remain on good terms with your former spouse.

If you are focused on ensuring that you and your family, particularly your children, are not damaged by your divorce, then take the time to work through these chapters and seek advice specific to your circumstances from a specialist family lawyer.

IT WILL GET BETTER, JUST HANG IN THERE

The information in this book has been gathered from many years of watching my clients, my friends and sometimes my family experience the trials and tribulations of divorce. I have seen many a silly mistake but also have experienced and assisted many people who have managed to have a dignified divorce – one that they have been able to look back on with pride when all the dust has settled.

In writing this book I have spent time speaking with clients, friends and family members to gain their insights on divorce and separation. There was one common theme from those who have been there – they all say, ‘It will get better, just hang in there.’

Splitsville will help you find your way to a place in the future where you too can look back on today and say, ‘I am okay.’

PART ONE

Where Do I Start?

Not till we
are lost
do we begin
to find
ourselves.

UNKNOWN

Am I ready to end it all?

I imagine most people in married or significant relationships think about throwing it all in at some point in time. For most of us, this is a fleeting thought that comes in and out the other side as we remind ourselves of all the good things associated with our relationships.

However, for others, the thought becomes a decision to end their significant relationship.

The decision to separate is not an easy one. You may be the person making this decision and may have spent some significant time thinking it through. I have met with clients who have taken five years or more to finally make the decision to end a long marriage. For others, this decision can be made very quickly. Sometimes the decision is not made by you but has been imposed on you unwittingly, leaving you in a state of shock and trying to understand why.

If you are reading this book and have not yet made the decision to separate, then I would strongly recommend you take your time in making this very significant decision. It shouldn't be a decision you make in the heat of the moment or after an argument.

A simple exercise to really consider the implications, advantages and disadvantages of the choice you are considering is comparing your future perfect world to your current reality.

PERFECT WORLD AND CURRENT REALITY

Find somewhere you can be alone and where you can have space to really think. Take a pen and paper and try to imagine what your life after separation will look like – you could choose a single imaginary day in your future life or perhaps a longer period such as a week. Write down how the day or week might work for you, your children and your family.

Next, consider why you are contemplating ending your relationship. Again, perhaps think of a recent day or week and on a separate note write down the matters that have been concerning you, your children and your family.

Now take out both notes. The first I call 'perfect world' – in other words, if everything went as you wished this is where you would hope to be in the future. The other note is best described as your 'current reality'. If you place these notes side by side, the 'current reality' on the left and the 'perfect world' on the right, you might start to see some patterns. There may be solutions in your perfect world to the concerns that exist in your current reality. Or there may not be solutions anywhere on the page.

Now, imagine what would happen if you didn't end your relationship. If you were to stay, what steps might you take to achieve some of what you see as your 'perfect world'?

On a third note, write a list of the steps you might have to take yourself; the changes you would need to make. Focus on personal change – what you might have to do and not what others might need to do. Don't evaluate whether you are willing to do these things, for now, just write them all down in a list. Sometimes there will be simple things like communicating differently with your spouse, while other changes might be more significant. Once you have a list of changes, try to delve a bit deeper – how will you do this? What would it look like? What would you actually have to do?

Before you consider whether your spouse might need to change at all, pause again and look at your list. Take the time now to evaluate, honestly, whether you are willing to commit to making change. The only way your relationship can improve is for you to commit to some form of change. That change could be an acknowledgement or acceptance, meaning that you choose to accept things as they are and to stop considering ending your relationship. This acceptance alone is a 'change' and can be a big change for some.

If you aren't willing to change, then this is a good sign that it is time to separate. After all, no matter your spouse's role in your current situation, you too have played a part and things will only change if you do.

If, on the other hand, you have managed to work through your list of necessary changes and you are willing to commit to some or most of these, start a similar list for your spouse. Again, try not to evaluate whether it is even possible for your spouse to do these things, just create a list. This list will be important and may form the basis of important conversations with your spouse around your desires to improve things or change them.

Remember, if you find yourself unable or unwilling to change, you can always separate in future. However, it is always worth trying to work things out before moving towards a final separation.

ASKING FOR HELP

If you want your relationship to continue, do seek assistance from a professional such as a family counsellor to help you and your spouse focus on the change that might need to be made.

A professional can assist you and your spouse to communicate, to openly discuss your concerns and, if you choose to end your relationship, to contemplate what the end of your relationship might mean and how you see your separation proceeding. Having these conversations together can be incredibly challenging, particularly if one or both of you are not ready for the separation. However, at least committing now to how you might work together after your separation to either co-parent or to divide your finances is a very important and powerful tool.

Even if you decide that you don't want your relationship to continue, I would still seek professional advice.

Divorce is said to be the second most significant grief process we can experience, second only to the death of a loved one. This means it is also one of the most significant decisions we will ever make. If you are still thinking about whether to separate, take the time to pause, to breathe and to grieve - this will be a difficult experience for both of you, but it will be more difficult if you rush into it.

The reality is that you
will grieve forever.
You will not 'get over'
the loss of a loved one;
you will learn to live with it.
You will heal and you will rebuild
yourself around the loss you have suffered.
You will be whole again
but you will never be the same.
Nor should you be the same nor would you want to.

ELIZABETH KÜBLER-ROSS

How will I cope?

Almost all of us have had our hearts broken at some stage in our lives. For me, it first happened when I was sixteen. I remember those feelings so well. I remember waking up each morning, feeling okay for those first few seconds before remembering what had happened, and then there was that sinking feeling in my stomach as I felt that heartbreak again. Of course, I was sixteen and in high school and had no understanding of what life in an adult relationship really meant and what pain could flow from the end of a marriage.

With now close to half of all marriages in Australia ending in divorce, and similar statistics for de facto relationships, more and more Australian adults are experiencing the heartbreak that flows from relationship breakdown.

When the end of your relationship is not your choice and comes as a surprise, you might think that this would be the most difficult situation of all in terms of managing the emotions that flow. Often, this is not the case – the grief associated with the loss of a significant relationship will be just as confronting whether the separation was your choice or not. Either way, you will feel fear, loss and sometimes anger. Perhaps the difference in this situation is that the person who has initiated the separation has been living their grief for some time during the relationship, while the person who has just been knocked sideways with the news of their impending breakup will be suddenly thrown into a deep state of shock.

However you have come to where you are today, it's important to understand the impact of emotion on your decision making.

As a family lawyer, every day I see good people at their worst. Grief can turn otherwise normal and sane people into chaotic and unpredictable disasters. The actions of you and your spouse early in your separation will affect how the two of you travel through your divorce and will have a lasting impact on your capacity to be friends at the end of all this.

Where most people go wrong is they immediately draw out their battle swords and start swinging. I think this is mostly done out of fear. Once we are in a difficult situation it is common to start to see the worst possible outcome first. We jump to conclusions and are often on edge, waiting for something terrible to happen.

Instead, think about where you want to be – imagine that 'perfect world' you mapped out in the last chapter – and focus on that as you go through the process. Remember, this too will pass, so just hang in there.

DEBBIE'S STORY

While I knew that divorce was the only option for our family, I was devastated. I come from the era that believes that when you marry it is for life, and that when things go wrong you need to deal with them. However, with the help of a psychologist I came to realise that it didn't matter what I did - I couldn't make it better.

I can remember waking in tears every day for about three months - not waking then crying, but actually waking in tears. This was not how my life was meant to pan out. My subconscious was working overtime. I felt like an incredibly sad, dismal failure, despite knowing rationally that I had done all that I could to save the marriage. I grieved for the loss of something that I held dear - my family was now not the traditional family.

THE DEATH OF A RELATIONSHIP

It is said that we experience grief at the end of a significant relationship in the same way and with a similar intensity to the grief suffered after the death of a loved one.

The Swiss-American psychiatrist Elisabeth Kübler-Ross was the first to propose that five stages of grief commonly are experienced as we adjust to the death of a loved one - denial, anger, bargaining, depression and acceptance. Her work has since been applied to the grief we experience during separation and divorce and other major personal losses. She proposed that not everyone experiences all five responses to a traumatic event and that the stages can be experienced in any order and also over and over again. Kübler-Ross also noted that her five stages of grief are not intended to be a complete list of all the possible emotions we can experience during a significant grief event. While Kübler-Ross' theory has been challenged, it still has application as a simple way of acknowledging and understanding the emotional stages we experience during a relationship breakdown.

STAGE OF GRIEF	DESCRIPTION	COMMON TRAITS SEEN DURING SEPARATION
Denial	We might know that our relationship is over, but we just can't believe it. We are in denial. We entertain fantasies of things still working out and look for glimmers of hope in situations around us. Denial is often associated with shock.	Denial is often experienced by the person who has been 'left'. They might be pretending nothing has happened, and repeatedly calling the other person even though that person has asked to be left alone. They will often talk about their former partner 'coming to their senses' and realising the error of their decision.
Anger	Anger is perhaps the easiest emotion to identify, but is expressed by different people in different ways. Anger can be directed at your former partner or at other people who might somehow be involved in the breakdown of your relationship. Some of us 'simmer' in anger, while others are explosive. Out of character behaviours are common at this stage of grief where even the most calm and rational people can do outlandish things as they express their anger.	Anger may be felt by the partner who has been 'left' and who feels that the decision to end the relationship was beyond their control. Anger can be directed at third parties, particularly family or perhaps a person involved in an affair with your former spouse. Anger is also often demonstrated by us trying to tell every man and his dog just how terrible our ex-partner is. We might also fall into the trap of sending hateful emails and texts, and should probably avoid the dreaded Friday night on Facebook with a bottle of wine as it can only end badly!

STAGE OF GRIEF	DESCRIPTION	COMMON TRAITS SEEN DURING SEPARATION
Bargaining	Bargaining and denial are often experienced hand in hand. We go from denial to bargaining and back again all in an attempt to find a way to 'fix' the relationship. We might promise, threaten or negotiate with our spouse in an attempt to get the relationship back on track. At this stage we are looking for any possible way, through almost any means, to preserve our relationship.	Many promises, threats and, at times, magical proposals might be made during the bargaining stage. Often a partner might 'plead' for the other partner to take them back, making promises that 'things will change'. At this stage help is sometimes enlisted from friends and family to try to make a partner 'see sense'. Long emails are exchanged reminiscing the 'good old days' in an attempt to pull at the heart strings. When this does not work, the next email will often be laden with threats of just how difficult that person's life is about to become if they keep going down the path of separation.

STAGE OF GRIEF	DESCRIPTION	COMMON TRAITS SEEN DURING SEPARATION
Depression	Depression is often associated with a feeling of hopelessness – the overall feeling that things will never be good again. Like anger, depression is expressed differently by different people. It might be physically with a loss of appetite and loss of sleep, or generally with a sense of feeling 'down'. For some of us it might mean an increase in drug or alcohol intake. This stage is perhaps the most difficult as, if the sense of hopelessness is able to take hold, it can be very difficult to know how to move forward and lift yourself out of that state.	It might be that you just want to lie in bed all day – one of those 'Bridget Jones' moments with lots of tissues, a dark room and a television. Someone in this stage of grief is often on the verge of tears and will seem disconnected. You might experience trouble sleeping and not have a desire to eat. It is also easy to try to mask the sense of hopelessness with alcohol or other drugs.
Acceptance	This final stage of grief is about accepting the end of your relationship and coming to terms with the loss. This does not mean that you are suddenly jumping around with glee, rather that you have reached a sense of peace and can start to look back on your relationship and see the good bits as well as the bad. This stage of letting go of the relationship may seem like it will never come and then suddenly one day you will realise you are there.	Once you can sit and talk about your former partner with some positivity, a smile on your face and even share some of the good times you will know you have reached 'acceptance'. It doesn't mean that you won't still have those feelings of hurt somewhere inside; however, they will be easier to manage. This stage will occur bit by bit and you may not even notice it happening, but you will feel better once you get there.

Where might you be in the grief cycle? Where you have been? There is every chance you have oscillated between phase one and two a few times before moving to phase three.

Now consider where your spouse might be in their own grief cycle. Think about some of their recent emotions and behaviours – are you better able now to understand why they might be acting the way they have been?

HOW TO GET OFF THE EMOTIONAL ROLLER COASTER ... FAST!

There is no 'right' way to grieve and no checklist you can follow. It is also not a linear process – you will move back and forth between the various stages of grief. You can, however, help yourself to move through this process as quickly as possible by following a few simple tips:

Remember it's okay to cry

Allow yourself to feel and experience emotion. This might initially include shock, sadness, anger or perhaps all of these at once. Whatever it is, allow yourself to experience it, but try to always control your actions as best you can. Remember, you will have days when you are feeling on top of the world only to wake the next day feeling like there is no light at the end of the tunnel.

Seek professional assistance

There has never been a better time to consult with a counsellor or psychologist to assist you through your grief. If you were sick you would see a doctor. If you have a legal dispute, you see a lawyer. So now that you are facing a significant personal event it is worth every cent to seek assistance to help you move through the emotional roller coaster as soon as possible so you can get on and enjoy your life.

Look to trusted family and friends

A great tip a client once told me was that she had an agreement with one friend who, no matter when or how, she could call just to talk. She knew that no matter how difficult things were, there was always one person who was willing to listen and offer advice. Find yourself a trusted support person, but don't overuse that person. Often the mere notion that a friend or family member will be available can be enough to help.

Set ground rules (and stick to them)

Set terms on how you will and won't engage with your spouse. You may not be able to reach agreements immediately about things such as your living and financial arrangements and you might be on the receiving end of lots of rude and hurtful communications. You can, however, set clear boundaries. For example, if you only wish to receive communication once a week by email (save for emergencies) then say so – but remember to stick to your own rules, too. While you cannot control how your spouse behaves, you can control yourself. So remember, if you are imposing any terms, be willing to abide by those same terms yourself.

Don't overreact

Try to keep things in perspective. When you have two people who are each experiencing grief about the same event and, to some degree, both of those people hold the other somehow responsible or at fault for their part in the failed relationship, we have a melting pot of grief just waiting to explode. This can make it very difficult to contain your actions but, if you can understand the stages of your own grief and, at the same time, the stage of grief that your spouse is experiencing, you will both be better able to move through your divorce and separation without causing harm to each other. You will be better able to interpret your partner's behaviour as an extension of their own hurt and pain instead of an act designed to cause you harm. This will hold you and your family in good stead for the future.

Be positive

Find yourself something to look forward to. Do something you have always wanted to do but could never do before. Join a new class, sporting team or social club. You don't have to go forever, but seeking out something new and different will help as you start to move forward. You might need to push yourself along occasionally.

Seek out information

Don't let a lack of knowledge lead you to feeling fearful. Meet with a family lawyer to seek specific information. Seek assistance from financial planners around things like budgeting. Look to your support network and gather information that will help answer your burning questions. While you may not like the answers, the sooner you can start to understand your future, the sooner you will start to find your way there.

Set small and achievable goals

By focusing on what you want to achieve day by day or week by week, you can celebrate your little wins while taking some of the pressure off. Keep a journal to map your progress – not to record the terrible things you are feeling, but the good things that are happening. There will always be something positive if you look hard enough.

Steer clear of the legal fight

An antagonistic and lengthy legal battle is a sure-fire way to keep you and your spouse in the early stages of the grief cycle for an unnecessarily long time. Couples who find themselves in the Court process will generally keep oscillating between bargaining, anger and depression, and will have lower chances of moving through the emotional aspects of their separation with dignity and their friendships intact. As I discuss in Part 3, it generally takes more than two years to reach the end of this process in our Family Court system. Try to take this into account when you are balancing your options early in your separation.

LOOKING TO THE FUTURE

Relationship breakdown is one of the most painful experiences many of us will have to face. The end of a significant relationship will mean change in many facets of your life and with this change comes a sense of loss, sometimes even the loss of your own identity. Having to let go of a significant relationship also affects your sense of security as you lose the support system of your marriage or relationship; a support system through which our worlds are often defined. This is often the case for people coming out of very long marriages that have spanned most of their adult life.

Your separation will reach beyond just you and your partner and will likely mean change for your children, your family, your friends, your business associates and your community of supporters.

Most people experiencing divorce say they 'just want it to be over'. What they are really saying is that they want the feelings and emotions to have passed. We often spend well over a year planning and organising a marriage, so expect a similar if not longer time frame for your divorce. Some studies have suggested that it takes at least three years to emotionally move on from the impact of your divorce. Some people can move forward much quicker than this, while for others the emotional impacts of their divorce almost never leave them.

While this book will guide you through your divorce and will help you move through the grieving process, one thing to keep in mind is to look to the future and not to the past.

There is little point in reliving the past – this often leads to apportioning blame for your failed relationship. Accept your role in things, recognise that you and your spouse may never see eye to eye on many things and start to plan your life into the future.

I sense we are programmed to identify all that is wrong in any situation as our default position. While it may be very, very hard to find, there will always be a silver lining if you can just start to see the world in a new light. No doubt it won't be there every morning when you wake up, but if you can spend some time each day finding something positive, something that creates optimism, you will move through your divorce with a lot more ease than some. To get started, give yourself something to look forward to. Do something you have always wanted to do but never could before. It might be a holiday, a dinner out or a new hobby – just something that you know you will enjoy that you can have in the back of your mind as something positive on the horizon. Remember, your life is precious and it's important to make the most of every single minute.

WENDY'S STORY

When I first met with Wendy, her husband had told her only two weeks earlier that their twenty-five-year marriage was at an end. He had met another woman and had been seeing her for almost four years. Wendy was devastated. I met with her for at least an hour. Through most of our appointment Wendy was crying and fluctuating between reason and clarity and despair about her future.

I chose not to focus on the legal details of Wendy's separation, but instead had a conversation about her and the sort of person she is. I asked about her goals in life and where she saw herself in twelve months' time. Wendy did not initially have answers to many of my questions, but over our hour together she was able to start formulating them.

A significant fear for Wendy was that she was going to have to leave her home. I could not provide her with immediate comfort around this issue as, from a legal perspective and on the limited information I had, I did have concerns that Wendy would not be able to afford to maintain her home and large mortgage in the long run.

Rather than having a detailed conversation about her home, Wendy and I instead chatted about her other options – if she had absolutely no choice but to leave her home, what could she do? This led us to a conversation around why she wanted to keep her home. It was not so much the physical structure itself, but more that it was very convenient - her three boys could walk to and from school and their friends were all nearby. Her work was just down the road. Her family had lived in that area for many years, and she felt 'at home' there. Part of her identity was tied to the local community and maintaining a connection to that area was essential. Through this conversation, I was able to understand why Wendy's home was so important to her.

Wendy left my office with some homework - to go away, take a deep breath and think carefully about how she visualised her life in twelve months' time, including where she might live and what she would be doing. I asked Wendy to write down as many ideas as possible before she started evaluating whether they were a good idea or not, and to write down ideas both for if she kept the home and if she left.

Wendy imagined that in a year she would be living close to her home, if not still in it. Her primary goal was to ensure that her boys had the best chance to complete their schooling and achieve to the best of their ability, and she imagined that her eldest boy had started university while her two other sons were still at high school.

Wendy also imagined she would be working a bit more than she was now. She was happy and was spending time with her friends and family on weekends. She spoke to me about occasionally having a pedicure - it might sound trivial, but Wendy had never had one before and for her it was something that symbolised her independence.

About four weeks later, Wendy contacted me again, ready to have a more detailed conversation about her legal options and to gain insight into what she thought she could and could not manage.

'YOUR LIFE IN A YEAR'S TIME'

You might be like Wendy and at the very first stages of your divorce, or you might be much further down the track. Either way I encourage you to give this exercise a go.

Find a quiet place, a pen and paper. Close your eyes and try to imagine yourself in a year's time. Imagine all the anguish and fear has passed. Imagine your divorce and separation are behind you. What does your life look like? Where are you? Who are you with? What are you doing? Write it all down.

What little changes might you make? What can you do now that you have not been able to do before? If you can try to find a few positives it will help you move forward.

Perhaps it is to paint a wall in your home a bold colour that you and your partner could never agree on before. Maybe it is to trade in that big car for the smaller, newer one you always wanted. Or maybe it's a pedicure, like Wendy. The list you are writing should be steeped in reality, not fantasy, but do allow yourself to dream just a little.

The items on this list will become your goals. They should be broad brushed, big picture and generally achievable. While I do believe we can do anything we set our minds to, now is not the time to add to your list that you plan on buying a small island (unless you genuinely can afford to!).

Once you have written how things might look in your life in one year (your goals) grab a new piece of paper. On this piece you are going to create a series of steps or tasks that will ultimately help you to achieve those goals.

In Wendy's case, one goal was to be living in her local area, preferably still in her home. So, some of the steps she set herself were:

- Find out just how much the bank might lend me so I can consider refinancing my mortgage;
- Look around at the cost of other properties in my area;
- Look at properties in other suburbs close by;
- Find out the cost of renting a house just like mine;
- Make enquiries with the local university to see whether I can rent out the lower floor of the home to students and what that might entail;
- Speak to local real estate agents to find out how much my home might sell for and how long a sale might take;
- And (perhaps my favourite) go and have a pedicure in the next seven days and then once a month until this is all sorted.

Try to do the same thing for yourself. Another example might be a goal that your younger children are able to move between you and your spouse with ease, and that you will all come together for important events in your child's life such as the first day of school. That might sound easy, but in the early stages of your separation it might be that you and your partner cannot speak civilly in the street, let alone walk your five-year-old daughter to school together.

So imagine your goal is to together take your five-year-old daughter to school on her first day next year (but right now you are not talking with your partner at all). Consider the steps it will take you to achieve that goal. Your list might include:

- Speak to a professional to understand how to move through my grief;
- Have an agreed plan for respectful communication between us as parents;
- Learn to separate my own emotion from my child's experience;
- Learn more about what my children may need when they are going through our divorce;
- Have a predictable parenting arrangement so I don't worry about when I will see my children;
- In a few months, meet my partner once every couple of weeks to talk as parents about how our children are going.

Once you have set these goals and steps, put them somewhere you can see them – in your phone or on your fridge. Maintaining a sense of positivity in an adverse situation takes courage. You will need courage to move through your divorce, but you can (and you will) come out the other side, perhaps a different person with a different kind of life.

Like a lot of things in life, it will often feel like three steps forward, two steps back. Remind yourself of this – set small and achievable goals, day by day or week by week. Keep a journal to map your progress; not to record the terrible things you are feeling, but the good things that are happening – there will always be something positive if you look hard enough. As my friend Debbie would say, 'When life gives you lemons, make a margarita!'

DEBBIE'S STORY

Divorce was probably the worst experience of my life, yet it has led me to change and grow and get to know myself so much better. Luckily for me, a couple of years before my divorce I had done some self-help work. I knew that I needed to feel the feelings that were welling up inside, but I also knew that I needed to nurture myself to get to a better place.

A little voice in my head told me that no matter what happened with the divorce settlement or how hard it seemed at the time, the sun was still going to rise in the morning and the tide was still going to ebb and flow. In the grand scheme of things my problems were insignificant, and I had trouble believing that The Universe was actually focusing on them when there were so many other people in so much more trouble than me. This helped bring things back into perspective.

I also decided to do something nice for myself every day – a bought coffee, ten minutes with a magazine, a nicely fragranced bath gel, or tea from one of my 'good' cups – just something that said, 'I love you and I am taking care of you.'

I also started to really look at the couples in the shopping centre ... most looked like they had an invisible shield between them – they rarely looked at each other or made eye contact. Often they didn't hold hands or physically touch in any way. Even though they were 'together' they didn't look like real couples and many didn't even seem to be enjoying themselves. All of a sudden I didn't feel so bad. I didn't want another 'bad' relationship. I started to list the good things about being single – looking only at what I wanted, leaving when I had had enough, never having to justify a purchase. Better to be single and happy than married and miserable. When I started looking at what I had gained rather than what I had lost, my whole thought process changed. I had come to the end of my acceptance journey.

At the time you are so caught up in the pain and uncertainty you really can't imagine that life will ever get back on track, but it can in some wonderful ways. It's nice to remember what you like and where you like to go, how you like to dress and keep the house, how you like to entertain and spend your leisure time. You still need to take the time to grieve and feel your loss, but always keep in the back of your mind the thought that things will get better – you will get stronger, you will sort out your finances and you will move on to new friends, new houses and new relationships when the time is right if you can hang onto an optimistic attitude and believe in yourself.

When life gives you lemons – make a margarita!

I may not
be there yet,
but I am closer
than I was
yesterday.

UNKNOWN

Where do I start?

If you've made the decision to separate, the next question is often 'Where do I start?'

Where possible, I recommend keeping your lives 'the same' in the short term to give yourselves time to properly plan where you might both go next. It is often not necessary for your finances to immediately change a day after you have separated. Similarly, you don't have to start organising living arrangements for your children two days after you have separated. Take your time, breathe and really think about what needs to happen immediately. There is every chance that almost nothing needs to change in the first few days.

If I could have the opportunity to sit down with a separating couple the day that their relationship has come to an end, I would talk to them about slowing down. I would see if it was possible for them to agree on arrangements for the next six weeks. Six weeks gives everyone a little bit of time to start to grieve, to start to consider their future and to start to remove some fear. If I suggested to you that you had to move house in only two weeks there is every chance that you would go into a state of panic or denial. However, if I said to you that you had about six weeks when nothing was going to change, when you could have security in your accommodation and your children's lives were not going to be any different, there is every chance that you would be able to relax just a little and start to focus on the future. I call this a 'holding pattern'. The sooner you and your partner can find a holding pattern the better. It is only a short-term solution, but one intended to allow both of you the time to start to grieve and the security to know that your lives are not going to turn upside down overnight.

DAVID'S STORY

David contacted me urgently one week. He had come home after work one day to find that his wife and his daughter had left their home. Their possessions were gone, some of the furniture was gone, and to David it appeared that his wife and daughter had moved without notice. She had turned off her phone and was uncontactable, and David was in a state of panic and shock as he tried to work out where she had gone. David knew that his marriage was coming to an end, but he had not been prepared to come home from work and find his wife and child had left.

I ended up assisting David for well over a year with the legal issues that flowed from his wife's decision that day to pack up their house and his daughter and leave. It turned out she had travelled south from Queensland to Victoria. David and his wife, Vicky, quickly found themselves in an expensive Court battle that required Vicky to return to Queensland with their young child only a few weeks after her move.

David and Vicky, up until that point, had had a reasonable marriage. The last few years had been tough in that they had not been talking or getting on well, but they were otherwise good, honest and nice people.

Vicky's decision that day to pack up and leave marked a significant fork in the road for this couple.

Had Vicky sat down with David and been able to express her fears, there is every chance that David would have agreed for her to go to Victoria and stay with her family for a few weeks to enable some time away and respite during the early stages of their separation. Vicky and David would have needed some agreement around David seeing their daughter, but I am confident that if David knew her trip was temporary he too could have seen benefit in the break. Instead, Vicky's decision to leave unannounced broke all trust between them. David would not trust Vicky on any issue after that day. I often wonder just how David and Vicky are going today – I expect they have as little to do with each other as possible, which is a terrible shame as that can only make things more difficult for their daughter.

CREATING YOUR 'HOLDING PATTERN'

When considering your holding pattern, try to focus on the next six weeks only. You should think about the following things yourself, and then take the time to talk with your spouse if you can to reach an agreement.

CONSIDERATION	A FEW OPTIONS	OTHER THINGS TO CONSIDER
Where will you both live?	Could you both stay in your home for a few weeks and sleep in separate rooms? Do you have alternative accommodation close by, like a rental or another home? Can one of you stay with friends or family? Could you each take turns to leave the home for a few days so one person does not feel like they are the one who has been displaced?	You should obtain legal advice before you make any significant decisions about whether to sell property. At this early stage, you are just looking to find a temporary arrangement to minimise conflict; you are not planning the entirety of the division of your financial matters.
How will you operate your finances for the next few weeks?	Can you leave things the way they were? Can you both agree not to make any significant change to the financial arrangements without first agreeing? Are there savings that you could divide between you so you both have some financial independence and security to obtain advice and plan your future? How will you pay the mortgage and other regular expenses?	At some point your finances will need to be separated, but this doesn't have to happen immediately. Where couples can do this gradually, I have seen lasting agreements form very quickly. By contrast, if someone withdraws funds without notice or rearranges bank accounts, it can immediately set the scene for mistrust and lead to significant conflict.

CONSIDERATION	A FEW OPTIONS	OTHER THINGS TO CONSIDER
What about your children?	What will you tell them? What, if any, changes will occur for them immediately? Do things need to change for them at all right now?	As parents, you both know your children better than anyone. Do consider their personalities, ages and emotional intelligence before having any conversations with them about your separation. Try to deliver a consistent message together that you both still love your children and your separation is not their fault. Remember that your children will also suffer grief as a result of your separation, so do everything you can to shelter them from your own emotions.
What other immediate things are concerning each of you?	Who else will you talk to about your situation? How might you tell family and friends? How will you communicate over the next few weeks?	Write a list of all the things that are worrying you, then try to reduce that list to the most pressing and important issues that you need some answers on. It might be as simple as knowing what your partner will be telling his friends and associates about your break up. It is helpful if you are both able to share a consistent story and keep intimate details private.

START AS YOU INTEND TO CONTINUE

The hardest thing to do after the initial shock of a separation is to put your emotions aside and try to have a conversation about some of the most important things in your life.

What most people don't realise is that the way they embark on this process affects the outcome. And your chances of future happiness will be far greater if you can act in a way that is consistent with your core values.

What do I mean by 'values'? Values are what you believe to be important. Our values determine our priorities and are often how we measure our success and happiness. When our lives align with our values we will generally feel happy. So, if we can consciously identify our values, we can make decisions and act in a way that is congruent with our values, which gives us a better chance of being 'happy'.

Beyond happiness in general, it is important to also try to understand your partner's core values for two reasons. First, you are about to enter negotiations and compromises with your partner over very significant issues, such as your children and finances. If you can understand what is important to your partner and create solutions that align with their values, you have a far greater chance of reaching a longstanding agreement that will meet the needs of both of you. Second, if you are going to remain friends and / or parent effectively together, part of your happiness will be affected by your partner's state of mind. There is little point in you setting goals, achieving them and moving forward if your former partner is left with an outcome that meets few of their needs, as your children will suffer. Instead, it makes sense that you work together to try to ensure you are both able to find a resolution that aligns with your personal values.

HOW TO IDENTIFY YOUR VALUES

If I ask you to list your 'core values' there is every chance you won't know where to start! And this won't have anything to do with your separation; it is just hard to put into words what really matters to each of us.

And so, I have a few exercises here that I use to help myself. I like to do this regularly, as it always intrigues me how things can change depending on what life wants to throw our way from time to time.

One way to identify your values is to look back on experiences in your life to identify the times when you were the happiest or perhaps the most proud and fulfilled. When were you most fulfilled during your childhood? Now consider your early adult life and more recent times. Consider your personal life and your career. What were you doing? Where were you? Who was with you? What else about those times made you feel happy?

Try to find around five occasions in your life when you felt happiness, pride and fulfilment. Write them down.

Now, using these experiences, try to look for common themes – these themes are often the link to your core values.

Another trick is to write down those things we often say / try and instil in our children or the young people in our lives. Those sayings that become part of our daily chat often represent the things that matter to us most.

Another exercise that I really like is to work through a list of common values to help me identify things that connect with me. I have created a list below of common core principles and values. You could use this to assist you in highlighting the things that matter to you. I find it easiest to strike through anything that doesn't matter to me first, then work through the list again and highlight the ones that I really connect with. Keep doing this same step until you can get it down to around five to ten words or phrases that really capture what matters to you most. And if it is not listed below, add it! The list is endless, really.

I like to do this exercise regularly with my family and colleagues in my team – it is interesting to see how our values can change over time and this a fun way to get to know each other more deeply.

Once you have done this activity for yourself, if you can, try to do the same thing for your former spouse.

Once you have your core values, write them down and then separately add those you identified for your former partner. If you have children, you could ask them to do the same activity.

COMMON CORE VALUES AND PRINCIPLES

You can use the list below to help identify what matters most to you. Start by crossing out anything that doesn't resonate with you. Then highlight the words or phrases that feel important. Keep repeating this process until you are left with around **five to ten** values that best reflect what matters to you right now.

If something important is missing, add it. This list is simply a guide.

Connection & Relationships

- Love
- Respect
- Trust
- Honesty
- Loyalty
- Kindness
- Compassion
- Friendship
- Connection
- Community
- Affection
- Belonging
- Quality relationships
- Understanding
- Unity

Family & Parenting

- Family
- Children's wellbeing
- Stability
- Consistency
- Safety
- Being present
- Positive role-modelling
- Shared responsibility

Personal Wellbeing

- Peace
- Calm
- Inner harmony
- Serenity
- Balance
- Rest
- Relaxation
- Health
- Vitality
- Joy
- Pleasure
- Fun
- Laughter
- Playfulness
- Lightness
- Mindfulness

Integrity & Character

- Integrity
- Accountability
- Honesty
- Ethical behaviour
- Responsibility
- Fairness
- Equality
- Tolerance
- Self-respect
- Courage
- Truth

Growth & Meaning

- Personal growth
- Development
- Learning
- Knowledge
- Wisdom
- Meaning
- Purpose
- Curiosity
- Creativity
- Intellectual challenge
- Potential
- Faith
- Spirituality
- Connection to something bigger

Independence & Security

- Independence
- Freedom
- Choice
- Autonomy
- Financial security
- Privacy
- Saving for the future
- Safety

Communication & How We Work Together

- Clear communication
- Listening
- Being heard
- Openness
- Collaboration
- Cooperation
- Problem-solving
- Flexibility
- Willingness to compromise

Effort, Direction & Achievement

- Achievement
- Action
- Initiative
- Determination
- Persistence
- Diligence
- Excellence
- Confidence
- Self-confidence
- Recognition
- Leadership

Structure & Practical Life

- Order
- Organisation
- Structure
- Planning
- Efficiency
- Simplicity
- Reliability
- Consistency

Connection to Others

- Generosity
- Giving
- Sharing
- Receiving
- Gratitude
- Appreciation
- Forgiveness
- Involvement

Joy & Energy

- Passion
- Excitement
- Adventure
- Challenge
- Celebration
- Movement
- Physical challenge
- Beauty
- Nature
- Play
- Fun for fun's sake
- Curiosity without purpose

ACTING IN LINE WITH YOUR VALUES

In the last chapter I wrote about how focusing on the future can help you move past your grief. Now I'd like you to focus on how you want to move from where you are now to that future state.

If family is important to you, then I would expect you would want to navigate this process with your family and friends close by. I'd also expect that you would want to make the transition as easy as possible for your children, which would involve maintaining a workable relationship with your spouse through your separation.

After your separation, you might want your children to be able to move between you and your spouse with ease, and for the two of you to come together for important events in your child's life, such as the first day of school.

Having worked with over 5,000 families over twenty-five years, I've found that the easiest way to achieve these goals is to ensure your behaviour remains values-based throughout your separation. Now I know how challenging this can be as you both move through the stages of grief; however, these five guidelines might help:

1. Think before you act, but always act calmly

As grief takes hold, expect to be at your worst. Expect the same from your partner. You will both be scared, emotional, fearful and unhappy. You will both express these emotions in different ways – think back to your relationship, as how you each dealt with emotions when you were together will be very similar to how you deal with them now. So, if your partner is someone who would hold onto their emotions, there is every chance that is how they will respond now. Similarly, if you are an explosive person there is every chance you will continue to act that way.

I have observed that my clients who were able to act with military precision – using calmness in the face of adversity to assess a situation and act when the time was right – were able to move through their grief at speed. If you are in the military, that precision comes from daily and repetitive training that is designed to ensure that when you face an emotional, fearful or stressful situation, your training kicks in and (hopefully) you act calmly and automatically. If only the skills learned through military training could be adopted by those making significant decisions through a divorce! Being able to act calmly during your divorce will often be anything but easy and is unlikely to be automatic.

Stop and think before you act, particularly if you are being asked to make a big decision. Try to be aware of moments when your emotions are getting the better of you and seek assistance from professionals, friends and family to keep you in check. Know your strengths and weaknesses. Chances are your former partner knows better than anyone how to push your buttons and you can do the same in return.

Take the time to think carefully before you speak, write or, in this day and age, text and tweet! Sometimes just sleeping on something can give you a whole new perspective by the next morning. You are aiming for a state of 'automatic calm response' even though the smoke may be billowing out your ears from time to time!

2. Listen twice as much as you speak

I've always loved the saying 'We have two ears and one mouth, so we should listen twice as much as we speak.'

When you are being asked to communicate with a former spouse about issues that are very important to you, it is perhaps the most difficult yet most important time to practise the concept of listening more than you speak. By listening I mean more than just hearing the words that are being said. You need to listen to the issues, concerns and fears that sit underneath those words.

Think about the stages of grief and try to understand the emotions that might be driving your spouse's words. If you can understand the emotions sitting beneath what is being said (you don't necessarily have to agree with them), then you will be better able to understand how you might meet their needs and, therefore, meet your own.

As you move through your separation you will need to negotiate and compromise with your spouse to find agreements on issues big and small. If you don't, you are ensuring a long-winded and conflictual battle that will cost thousands of dollars and cause significant emotional harm. There is power in silence and much to be gained from listening and really hearing, understanding and acting accordingly.

3. Don't believe everything you hear

Don't get me wrong; listening is incredibly important but, at the same time, don't believe every single thing you hear. Family, friends and even the local real estate agent will all have something essential that they feel they must share to assist you with your divorce. Carefully consider whether these helpful tips really will assist you.

So often I am told by clients that their children have told them something and all of a sudden that information becomes gospel. For example, 'Johnny tells me that he doesn't want to see his mother on weekends any more,' is suddenly interpreted by Johnny's father as somehow illustrating a truth that Johnny doesn't want to spend time with his mother. This statement from a young child experiencing his family breaking apart could mean many different things, but very rarely means that he does not want to see his mother.

If you are able to listen but also assess why something is being said by those around you, including your children, you will be more able to move through your divorce with minimal conflict. Don't get me wrong, children often say things that are very important and should be given much credence, but just like you, your children are trying to navigate the tricky world of separation. They too will say things without the meaning that is perhaps later applied to them by adults who are carefully listening for signs that their children's wellbeing might be affected by the divorce.

4. Let a few goals go through to the keeper

When I talk to clients about communicating with their spouse, I often say, 'Don't be afraid to let a few go through to the keeper.'

Once couples find themselves in a legal process, there seems to be a misconception that every email or text message suddenly has to be responded to so that the 'truth' is known. This is simply not the case. It is ultimately highly unlikely that the chain of emails and texts will ever be read by anyone other than you and responding can often cause more angst than is necessary, as well as prolong the grieving process.

You don't always have to have the last word. It also does not matter if you 'give in' on a few things that are perhaps not so important to you but more important to your spouse. Work out what really matters to you and focus on the big picture – if it is really important to you that you share the costs of your children pursuing their dreams, then don't compare every cent each of you spent that month on tennis lessons, uniforms, rackets and balls. Swings and roundabouts, as they say!

Avoiding conflict over things that 'just don't matter' is often one of the hardest things to do during your divorce. If you can let a few goals through to the keeper, you will remain focused on the bigger issues at hand and ensure unnecessary conflict is minimised.

To achieve this, try to keep communication verbal where possible – we interpret so much from the way something is said rather than the words that are used. If conversations are not productive, then try to reach agreement around the type and frequency of communication. A multitude of emails and texts each day is rarely going to be helpful to either of you.

And, if you do receive an email or text that you consider hurtful, rather than responding in kind, pause and try to understand whether that message might just be part of a stage of grief. Rather than answering, perhaps leave it for a few days and see if the situation can improve without you needing to respond. Just because someone has said something, or even written it down, does not make it true. And, more importantly, who will ever read it anyway?

At times it might be worth engaging the services of a counsellor to assist in facilitating conversations with a view to forming agreements, rather than simply engaging in a tit for tat 'trial by text message'.

5. Put your children first

This one sounds easy, right? Well, it's not. You will be navigating a path that involves times of emotional turmoil, and I can promise you it will become more difficult than ever to put your children's needs before your own. It will be near impossible if you feel that your former partner is constantly putting his or her needs before the needs of you and your children.

However, if you and your former partner can focus on the needs of your children, you can be assured that your children will not be damaged by your separation. They will not be placed at risk of poorer outcomes before they have even begun to navigate their way through our complicated world as they find their way to adulthood.

These guidelines, as well as those in the chapter on parenting arrangements, all allow you to put your children's needs above your own.

In general, try to treat your partner the way you would want to be treated (noting that this will not always be so easy!).

If you find that you cannot sit together and have a sensible conversation, you could also consider:

Using a facilitator

Sometimes family and friends are your best supports at these difficult times. If there is a close confidant that you both trust and who you think could act impartially and help you and your spouse through a difficult conversation, then ask them to come and assist. Alternatively, use a family counsellor or mediator. You can get urgent assistance from a qualified professional to assist you and your spouse to have this conversation. A great service in Australia is the Family Relationship Advice line provided by the Australian Government. You can call 1800 050 321 or visit www.familyrelationships.gov.au to find a professional in your area and access lots of great information and support. A professional will be independent, is trained in how to manage emotion and conflict, and will help both of you to stay on track and reach a resolution.

If all else fails, write it!

While not always ideal, putting things in writing can be a great way to communicate when you are emotionally unable to communicate in person. Be aware of the limitations that flow from using written communication. Something like 95 per cent of our understanding of communication comes from non-verbal cues, and email and text have none of these cues. Emails sent during work hours are also notoriously brief and blunt. Advances in technology also mean that we can be bombarded at all hours with emails, texts and other messaging systems. If you are going to use the written word to negotiate such significant issues, be clear in your message and set terms regarding your availability to consider any responses. Think about the tone of your communication and don't include spiteful comments, as you will only receive the same in return. Consider asking a friend to read your communication before you send it if you are concerned about the tone. There are several great apps designed to help partners communicate after separation that, thanks to the AI bots, have 'tone meters' built in, and they work a treat in those difficult moments!

How you behave in these very early stages of your separation will have a significant impact on where you end up and how quickly (or slowly) you might get there. However, most of the clients I see have not had the opportunity to discuss with their spouse how they would like their separation to proceed. Instead it is more often the case that, after the decision to end a relationship has been made, the communication between a couple disintegrates. It is from this point that I see couples reach a fork in the road that can determine very quickly the type of divorce they will experience.

By choosing at the beginning how you would like your separation to proceed, acting in line with your values and using the four guidelines mentioned earlier, you will have a much better chance of experiencing an amicable separation, even if it feels impossible at the time.

I don't have time to worry about
the people who don't like me,

I am too busy
loving
the people who
love me.

UNKNOWN

How do I tell everyone?

What do I tell everyone,' and 'what will people say?' are often two of the first concerns that come up for people once the initial shock of the separation has worn off. Again, my advice here is to take your time, work with your partner (if you can) to decide how you want to break the news and what you want to share, and keep the end in mind - the way in which you tell your family, friends and others about your separation can have a significant impact on your relationship with your spouse going forward. If you let emotions like anger come into these communications, it can make the subsequent legal process far more difficult than it needs to be.

WE NEED TO TELL THE KIDS

Telling your children of your separation is no doubt one of the most significant and difficult conversations you will have. Often this conversation occurs just after you have decided to separate and when you are both in the throes of sorrow, hurt and pain. Because of this, it's very easy to get it wrong. Most commonly, I have seen the aggrieved parent take it upon themselves to break the news to their children and to ensure that the children understand in intimate detail the reason why mum and dad are separating. I have seen children who have heard all about their mother or father's affair and how it is all her or his fault that their parents have separated.

Remember that while the end of a relationship is very difficult on the adults involved, it is often more difficult on the children involved. Children, depending on their ages, will understand in different ways the separation of their parents, and will almost always experience some level of hurt. Many children will also feel somehow responsible for the end of their parents' relationship.

It isn't always possible to curate a conversation with your children after separation. Sometimes things happen quickly, kids have seen or been a part of difficult circumstances and, at times, have had to leave a home quickly for safety. Whatever the circumstances, it is important to give space for your children to ask questions, explain their experiences and feel heard. It is equally important to be mindful with the answers and information you give, to try to shelter them from adult conflict where you can.

This is why, no matter how difficult your separation is for you, it is essential that you try to separate your own emotions and be available to support your children, who will also be grieving the change in your family. You and your spouse should work together to offer support to your children where you can. It is best if you can, together, send a clear message for your children that it is okay for them to keep loving both of you in just the same way.

Here are five tips on how to have the hard conversation:

1. **Try to agree with your partner on when you will talk with the children.** It's important to break this news together if you can, but if you can't, that's okay. Just try to be clear on who is telling the kids what information and when so you are both ready to support them.

2. **Take into account the ages of your children.** If they are very young this conversation should focus on letting them know everything will be okay. If they are teenagers you might need to talk more deeply about the experience for them.

3. **Don't involve your children in adult issues, such as financial or personal issues that have led to your relationship ending.** Children do not need to know and, in most cases, cannot understand the varied issues that will have led to the end of your relationship. There is every chance you don't really know either! Children need to be reassured that, despite the breakdown of your relationship, you will continue to be good parents who will love them and that they will continue to be a priority in your life. Younger children will need to be reassured that it is not their fault that your relationship has come to an end. This is one of the hardest things for most parents after a separation, particularly if you feel that you are the innocent party, or the separation was not your choice or out of your control. Keep in mind that you are both going through the grieving process, so seek professional assistance with your own emotions rather than imparting your feelings on your children.

4. **Don't say bad things about your partner.** Children are a biological product of their parents. Children therefore understand that they are, in essence, half their mother and half their father. By slighting or denigrating a child's mother or father you are, at the same time, slighting that child. Even if this isn't your intention, this will cause emotional harm to your children and affect their capacity to grow into emotionally healthy adults.

5. **Do remember that every family is unique.** Don't compare yourself to other families or friends in your situation. A relationship brings two people together with their own views, beliefs and values. These flow into your parenting style. It is important to try to make decisions that suit your family based on what you and your former partner consider to be the best for your children. You both know them better than anyone else.

YOUR SEPARATION – A CHILD'S PERSPECTIVE

Sarah was seven years old when her parents decided to end their marriage. She was a happy young girl, doing well at school with a good circle of friends. Sarah's mum, Jane, worked part time and was responsible for getting Sarah to and from school most days of the week. Sarah's dad, Ken, was an engineer who worked quite long hours and generally would leave for work around 7am each day and not be home until dinner time in the evenings.

Sarah knew her parents weren't very happy. She had heard them yelling at each other for months. She just hoped that the yelling would stop and they could go back to how everything used to be.

One day Sarah came home from school and her parents sat her down and said to her that they were getting a divorce. Sarah did not know what that meant but had heard from some of her friends at school that a divorce was a bad thing. Sarah's mum told her that she was moving to a new home. Sarah's dad told her that she would now be living in two homes.

Sarah could see that her mum was really sad when she was telling her that she was moving home. Her dad seemed happier when he told her what was happening. What Sarah couldn't understand was why her mum and dad didn't want to live in the same house with her any more.

She went to bed that night and thought long and hard about all the things she had done wrong that year. She cried and cried and wished that she'd just been better so that her mum and dad were still together.

NICOLE'S STORY

As a child, you put all your hope and faith into your parents. You're taught to believe that your parents' love for you is unfaltering, and that they will always do what's best for you. While this may be true, going through your parents' divorce can be an earth-shattering experience, where you find yourself questioning everything you believe. Fortunately for me, I had a solid Christian upbringing to ground my faith in and spent most of the ordeal making a mental list of things that I would, and would not, do if I were the parent in their situation. After ten years, I've managed to organise my mental list into three main categories.

Communication

Contrary to popular belief, human beings are not mind-readers. However, a child will notice tension between their parents. So to those parents who want to 'shield their child', please do your children a favour and tell them what's going on. However, it's not necessary to fill them in on all the gory details. Sometimes a simple explanation and some reassurance of your continued love for them is all they need.

Privacy

A marriage is a private relationship between a husband and wife. In the same way, a divorce should also be kept private, save for some professional advice if necessary. I am by no means saying that you shouldn't reach out for support from family and friends. However, there is never any need to tell every Tom, Dick and Harry why you're getting divorced. If you're wondering why, the reasoning is simple. First, it can be humiliating for both partners to have the most private details of their marriage circulating in the community. Second, and probably more importantly, you run the risk of your children hearing about their own family problems (perhaps in more detail than you'd like) from someone other than their own parents, which can be devastating for them.

Respect

A divorce is, more often than not, a very contentious experience. Both parents will probably feel that they are 'right', and that they are the victim. There is no need to share this with your children. It is understandable if parents are not on amicable terms with each other, but talking about each another in a degrading (and downright rude) way in front of your children never helps. By doing so, you place them right in the middle of your conflict, you pit them against either parent, and you also give them permission to repeat the things that you've said to others. As a side note, remember that your children are never your spies, and you should not be using them as a means of gaining information about your ex-partner.

Divorce is not always the ideal environment for children, and should be avoided where possible. However, where it can't be avoided there is always potential for a smooth transition for parents and children - the experience does not have to be as negative as the stories you hear. The most important thing to remember is that children are very impressionable, and the way that they perceive relationships and marriages can have significant implications for them later on. Do not let them lose hope in the possibility of a happy marriage – the best way to do that is to show them that love still exists in your relationship with them, even if it doesn't with your spouse.

Finally, try to shelter your children from the comments and thoughts of your family and friends. There is nothing more harmful for a child than hearing either of their parents described in a negative way.

As a parent, you can have a profound impact on your children. This is certainly the case during separation. There are many resources available that can assist you in talking to your children and supporting them at this difficult time. Also consider the resources that already exist around you and your family that can assist your child. This might include school counsellors, teachers, church and other family supports.

WHAT ABOUT OUR FAMILY AND FRIENDS?

Just like your children, it is helpful if you can have an agreement around the message you will deliver to your family and friends. Again, it is best if you can avoid sharing intimate details of the reasons for your relationship breakdown with everyone around you. Pick your confidants carefully – it is important that you have supports around you with whom you can share your thoughts and feelings, but they don't need to include the parents of every one of the kids at your children's school!

Also don't choose your husband's or wife's parents as your confidants. You cannot expect your parents to do much other than side with each of you so don't expect anything more from them by placing them in difficult situations.

No matter how much it hurts, try to keep your emotions contained and share your thoughts only with a few of your closest friends and family. The more information you allow to be shared to your greater network, the more damage you and your family will likely suffer in the long run.

WHAT ABOUT WORK?

You may also want to consider informing your workplace or employer of the change in your circumstances. There is no requirement to do this and again it will depend on where you work and your relationships within your workplace. Being upfront about what is occurring can be a good idea, particularly if you need some additional support or even some personal leave. You may also want to change account or superannuation details and perhaps, later down the track, your name on employment records. Again, take your time with this decision. It may also assist in being upfront with your employer as it will help with future discussions about any changes you might want to make in your work hours or in seeking more flexible arrangements.

Like every other aspect of your separation, how you tell people should be guided by your values. No matter the reasons for your separation, remember that, just as your relationship was private, your separation is also a private affair. Also, if you have children, remember that your partner is also a parent and, as parents, the two of you will remain a part of each other's lives for some time to come. So, the more respect you and your partner can maintain during these early stages, the more dignified your divorce will be and the easier it will be to move forward into a new life.

PART TWO

Twenty Years of Marriage Condensed into Three Legal Issues

Just remember
that the
future
comes one day
at a time.

UNKNOWN

Welcome to the minefield of Family Law

FASTEN YOUR SEAT BELTS, THIS WILL BE A BUMPY RIDE!

Now that you've made the decision to separate, have agreed on an initial holding pattern and have thought about what to tell your children, friends and family, it's time to start getting your head around the minefield that is Family Law.

So what is the 'Family Law'?

Almost every Australian separated couple, whether married or de facto, will find that the legal matters arising after the breakdown of their marriage are dealt with by application of the law as set out in the Family Law Act 1975 Cth ('the Act').[1] This piece of legislation is over fifty years old now, although it tends to be updated almost annually.

As far as the Act is concerned, there are generally three areas that affect most separating couples:

1. Matters relating to parenting and arrangements for children
2. The division of a couple's financial affairs, including income and property
3. The dissolution of a marriage (your divorce)

While there are other more specific and unique matters that can arise upon the breakdown of a relationship, these tend to be the three main areas where separating couples find themselves dealing with the law.

'I JUST WANT WHAT IS FAIR!'

When the Act came into effect in 1975, it resulted in a significant change for our society in terms of how separation and divorce were approached.

Most importantly, the 'no-fault' divorce system was introduced. In essence, this means that, to seek a dissolution of a marriage, there is no need or benefit in

1 The legislation and operation of the Family Courts in Western Australia is slightly different from that in other states around Australia. The effect of that legislation, though, is largely the same as the Family Law Act 1975 (Cth). No matter where you live, you should get advice from a Family Lawyer specific to your circumstances.

trying to establish that a party to a relationship is 'at fault'. It is only necessary to show that there has been an 'irretrievable breakdown of the marriage'. This was a significant change as it had previously been necessary to provide evidence of one party's guilt of adultery or abuse before a divorce could be granted. This legislative change put a lot of private detectives out of work! This 'no fault' concept flows through to the application of the Family Law Act in relation to both parenting and property matters.

This can create a lot of distress for clients who 'only want what is fair'. The issue is that, like beauty, fairness is in the eye of the beholder, and there is a strong chance that what you consider to be 'fair', what I consider to be 'fair' and what your partner considers 'fair' will all be different. When it comes to the application of the Family Law Act there is no concept of 'fairness'. Rather, there are a series of, at times complicated, legal principles that have been set out by our legislators that the Family Law Courts apply. This creates the law that I as a family lawyer try to apply to your personal circumstances.

This means that someone being 'at fault' will rarely have any impact on the legal outcome of your property division or parenting regime. This is important to understand and remember from the outset. Too often I see clients getting stuck and distracted in legal negotiations because their spouse has 'done the wrong thing' in their relationship. There is likely to be a significant distinction between your personal values and beliefs and legal principles. There is no 'fairness' step or principle that I have found in the Family Law Act, so it is important to try to separate, very early on, what you consider to be 'right' or 'wrong' and what the law considers to be appropriate or irrelevant.

MARRIED OR DE FACTO DOES IT MAKE ANY DIFFERENCE?

There are generally two types of relationships governed by the Family Law Act – marriages and de facto relationships.

A marriage is perhaps the easiest to define and understand, as a married couple will have a certificate that evidences the day on which they entered the legal union of marriage. You were either married or not – you can't be 'sort of married'.

De facto relationships are more difficult, as two parties to a relationship can see it in a very different light. What one person considers to be a committed relationship, almost like a marriage (albeit without the certificate and ceremony), the other can consider an uncommitted relationship, or not even a 'relationship' at all.

Where the presentation of a marriage certificate is enough to establish that you were married and thereafter enliven the necessary sections of the Family Law Act that might relate to the division of your property, the difficulty with de facto relationships is that there is very rarely such clear evidence of an intention to enter into a committed relationship. Often de facto relationships grow and change over time. After a separation, it can sometimes be very difficult to look back in time and pinpoint the exact moment that you consider your relationship went from just 'a relationship' to a committed de facto relationship. In some states in Australia you can 'register' your de facto relationship but, in practice, this seems uncommon.

The general legal test for determining whether a couple are in a de facto relationship is whether you have been 'living together on a genuine domestic basis' for more than two years.

Sounds very fancy, of course, and the terms 'genuine domestic basis' are broad brushed and intended to refer to the many, varied types of relationships that exist in our society. There is a list of matters that will be considered to determine if a relationship is a 'de facto' relationship, including:

- The length of the relationship
- Whether the couple were living together
- Whether a sexual relationship existed
- The financial arrangements that were in place
- The way the couple owned and used their property
- The degree of commitment to a shared life
- If the relationship was registered
- The care arrangements for any children
- The couple's reputation and public aspects of their relationship

THE 'TWO-YEAR RULE' FOR DE FACTO RELATIONSHIPS

Once you have established that a relationship is a de facto relationship you then need to show that it lasted more than two years before the Family Law Act can assist you. In other words, unless you were living together as a couple, 'on a genuine domestic basis', for at least two years, it is unlikely you will be able to pursue a property settlement. I call this the 'two-year rule'.

There seem to be many misunderstandings about the required length of a de facto relationship when it comes to Family Law. I have had some lengthy debates about this one with friends who seem to be convinced that after six months the law will take effect. This is simply not the case (save for two exceptions below). Where I think a lot of us get confused is that there are different definitions of the term 'de facto relationship' that can be used by different government departments and agencies. For example, the Department of Immigration will consider a relationship where a couple have been living together for only six months to amount to a de facto relationship when they are assessing eligibility for some visas. Similarly, Services Australia consider any couple relationship from the time you begin to live together as a de facto relationship for their purposes.

There are two main exceptions to the two-year rule:

- There is a child of your de facto relationship; or
- One of you has made such a significant contribution to the assets of the relationship that it would be unjust if Orders were not made. An example of this might be that the relationship lasted only eighteen months, but one party made a significant lump sum payment, say $100,000, to reduce the other spouse's mortgage. In this circumstance it may be appropriate that Orders are made to divide the existing property between the couple even though their relationship did not meet the usual two-year threshold.

ESTABLISHING THAT THERE WAS NO RELATIONSHIP

During a difficult separation there can be benefits for a party to a de facto relationship to try to establish that there was no de facto relationship at all – this means that the Family Law Act would not apply and that couple may not be able to seek a division of their financial affairs in the usual way. If you consider yourself to be in this category, you will need to seek specific advice from a specialist family lawyer as the process of proving or even disproving a de facto relationship can be an expensive and burdensome one.

YOUR RELATIONSHIP TYPE AND THE LAW

Generally, the law is the same whether you are married or in a de facto relationship:

1. When it comes to your children, it does not matter if you are married or in a de facto relationship – the law is the same.
2. When considering your financial affairs, if you are in a de facto relationship you need to establish that it lasted more than two years. In that case the law applies to you in almost an identical way as it does to married couples.

3. If you were in a de facto relationship for less than two years, you should seek legal advice from a Family Law specialist specific to your circumstances.

KEEP YOUR EYE ON THE BALL

As we work through the legal principles that relate to your separation, keep in mind the goals and values you have identified for you and your partner. While the law will not necessarily take those into account, you and your spouse can.

The best settlement options find a balance between a couple's legal rights and entitlements and their personal goals, needs and values. This balance is only possible with settlements that are reached through constructive discussion and negotiation outside the court process. By contrast, families who find themselves before the Family Courts are left with the pure application of legal principle, which will mean that very little importance will be placed on the goals and desires of the separating couple.

No matter what,
be the parent
that your child
needs.

UNKNOWN

Who gets the kids?

THE FIRST LEGAL ISSUE

There is no end to the research that shows children who experience the conflictual divorce of their parents during childhood have lower levels of success in life.

At the beginning of this book, I told you the story of Anne, her partner, Bill, and her son, James. I hear from Anne every couple of months and I know that her separation from Bill and the subsequent legal process she endured has had a lasting effect on her life. She spent over $200,000 with various lawyers and other professionals during her legal dispute. If Anne were undertaking the same process now, I expect her legal costs would have been more than half a million dollars. More importantly, though, and what is impossible to quantify, is the emotional and personal damage that Anne has suffered – she lost her career, her identity and her confidence. Anne's life changed and it will be a long time before it is back on track.

Then there is James. While Anne is now out of the legal process, James is still negotiating a small, bumpy bridge every other week that is the path between his parents. His parents don't talk, they don't meet in public and they communicate only by email. James will never experience the joy of seeing the two people most important to him sitting in a school assembly or watching him compete in sport - Anne and Bill simply cannot be near each other.

Anne and Bill's story is not unique. Almost every parent I have worked with in the Court process comes out scarred or changed in some way. Those parents barely talk with each other in the end, and their children suffer as a result.

What is important to remember is that it is not the divorce of parents that causes this harm; it is the ensuing conflict. If you allow your children to experience the conflict that exists between you and your partner, whether overtly or subtly, you are harming them in a way that cannot be repaired.

If, however, you shield your children from harm, ensure they are sheltered from adult disagreements and enable them to move fluidly between your households, then it is unlikely that your divorce will have any lasting impact on their adult lives. This can only occur when you as separated parents maintain trust and respect in each other.

Post-separation parenting arrangements will always be very difficult for both parents and children. What is essential is that you ensure that you create a childhood for your children, no matter where they are living, that gives them the best chance to achieve their dreams and live their lives to the fullest.

As far as the law is concerned...

The arrangements for your children after your separation and other issues that relate to their care and welfare are ultimately governed by the Family Law Act.[2]

The Act sets out the 'objects' or goals of the law as it relates to parenting matters 'to ensure that the best interests of children are met, including by ensuring their safety'.[3]

BUT I HAVE RIGHTS, TOO! DON'T I?

Perhaps the most important legal principle to understand when it comes to your children is that, as a parent, you do not have a legal right to spend time with them. You do, however, have responsibilities and duties to provide for and nurture your children.

This concept may seem at first blush to be 'upside down' – how could children have rights? But if you give it some thought, it does make a lot of sense.

The paramount principle the Court applies when considering arrangements for children is whether those arrangements are in the 'best interests' of a child or children. The issue is that what is 'best' for a child is another discretionary concept that two parents may or may not agree on.

2 For the specific legislation relating to parenting matters, see Part VII of the Family Law Act 1975 (Cth).

3 See Section 60B of the Family Law Act 1975 (Cth).

In the legal sense, a Court will consider the following when determining if something is or is not in the 'best interests' of a child:

1. The need for the arrangements to promote the safety of the child, and any person caring for the child, so as to protect them from being subjected to, or exposed to, family violence, abuse, neglect or other harm;
2. Any views expressed by a child, taking into account the child's maturity or level of understanding;
3. The child's developmental, psychological, emotional and cultural needs;
4. The capacity of the parents to provide for the child, including the child's developmental, psychological, emotional and cultural needs;
5. The benefit of a child having a meaningful relationship with both of the child's parents, where it is safe to do so;
6. Anything else that is relevant to the particular circumstances of that child;
7. Any history of family violence / current Domestic Violence Orders; and
8. The rights of Aboriginal and Torres Strait Islander children to enjoy their culture.

These factors are listed at s60CC of the Family Law Act and are an essential part of that Act when it comes to parenting matters.

The Family Law Act is continually updated and amended to better guide families to formulate the living arrangements for children after separation.

In May 2024, there were some significant changes to the law, which saw the removal of the presumption that both parents should share 'Equal Shared Parental Responsibility' for their children. This provision previously meant that parents should have, where appropriate, the ability to together make important decisions in relation to their children. This did not mean that there was any presumption that children spend equal time with each parent; however, this was not clear within the legislation.

There is no law that says children should spend equal time with their parents. The Family Law Act provides for the 'best interests of a child' to be the framework applied when determining what arrangements should be put in place for children.

Since the 2024 changes, when considering the decision-making responsibility of parents, the Court will consider what is in the children's 'best interests'. The law encourages parents to consult each other about major long-term decisions for their children (if it is safe to do so).

You might start to see a common theme emerging in terms of the legal principles and parenting issues – there is a very strong weight placed on the importance of children having meaningful relationships with their parents, where it is safe for them to do so.

This focus is not surprising. Research consistently shows that understanding where we come from – and feeling connected to our parents and family – plays an important role in the development of our identity as human beings.

SHOULD I LEAVE IT TO THE COURTS?

As I mentioned in the last chapter, one of the difficulties with the pure application of the Family Law Act is that the intricacies of your family and your children, including your values, routines and goals, will not necessarily feature in the legal considerations. While a Judge will take all the principles into consideration, this will not always take into account, in the way you might prefer, your children's ages, needs, maturity and temperament.

This is why you and your partner, as the parents of your children, are the people best placed to make such significant decisions for them. Most parents are able to negotiate arrangements for their children after separation without the assistance of the Family Courts. Don't be afraid to try different things and custom-design your parenting arrangements to suit your family.

Most separated parents – those who can cooperate, communicate and generally get on – will make decisions about their kids together in some way, shape or form. We lawyers call this 'shared or joint parental responsibility'. If you plan on formalising your parenting agreement in a legal way (I will tell you more about how to do this in Part 3), you will generally want to include a provision for you and your partner to have 'shared or joint parental responsibility'.

POST-SEPARATION PARENTING ARRANGEMENTS

Are you French or German? Cooperative parenting

Let me tell you about France and Germany – both beautiful nations right next to each other, with France to the south and Germany to the northeast. The French, of course, live in France – they have their own language, culture, customs and delicious cuisine. The Germans, of course, live in Germany with their own language, culture, customs and equally delicious, but heartier, cuisine. Every single day German people cross the border between France and Germany to visit friends, go to work or even go on a holiday. As they cross the Rhine River they can take with them their language, customs, culture and cuisine. Similarly, every day a Frenchman will cross the very same border to spend time in Germany, bringing with them their language, customs, culture and croissants. Even though they have different cultures at their core, people in France and Germany who live close to the border are able to live in harmony due to their mutual acceptance, understanding and respect.

In fact, the governments of France and Germany have been working together for many years now to help their citizens move between their two nations. To make it easy for their people they have signposts written in both French and German. They have joined with other nations to create a single currency so their people can easily spend money in both countries. They have relaxed border control so their citizens are encouraged to move back and forth as they please.

But you see, when the Frenchman comes to Germany he remains a Frenchman. He is not asked to leave his language and culture at the border. He is encouraged to bring it all with him and soak up some German culture while he is there. He remains a Frenchman but is able to easily move between his country and that of his neighbour, enjoying the best of what each nation has to offer.

In the post-separation parenting world, France and Germany are just like mum and dad, and their citizens are their children. Parents who are able to cooperate after their separation – allowing their children to move with ease between their nations and bring with them the language, culture and customs from the other parent's home – are engaging in cooperative parenting. This is the ideal for children of separated families and will ensure your children do not suffer as a result of your separation.

You must be French or German! High-conflict parenting

If we go back, however, to the time of World War II, it was a very different scene for the people of France and the people of Germany. Their nations were fiercely at war against each other. There was no freedom of movement between the two nations. The bridges that once had allowed the people of each country to move back and forth with ease suddenly became strategic strongholds, riddled with danger for anyone trying to cross. The French were not welcome in Germany and the Germans were not welcome in France. If a Frenchman found himself in Germany he would do his best to hide his language, culture and customs to ensure his survival. Similarly, the German in France would leave his language, culture and customs at the border in an attempt to blend in and survive.

Think of Anne, Bill and James. Let's imagine Anne is France and Bill is Germany. James is living each week of his life in a war zone between the nations of his parents. He has to negotiate a strategic border between his parents every other weekend. His parents cannot assist him with this and have engaged professionals at a local children's contact centre as a form of border control just to ensure that the transition from Anne to Bill even happens.

When James lives with his mum in France there are a set of rules, customs and behaviours that James has come to know. But when James goes to live with Bill in Germany there are different rules, customs and behaviours. James can cope with the differences, but what he cannot cope with is Bill demanding that he leave the things he has come to know with his mum at the door. James cannot talk about his 'other life' with mum, he cannot bring his toys and he cannot share his experiences. He hides a large part of himself and leaves behind everything that he associates with his mum before he enters his dad's world. James is living in a war zone of high-conflict parenting and there is nothing he can do other than protect himself. James will initially protect himself by withdrawing and being very careful with his interactions with both of his parents to ensure he does not become the subject of their complaint. He will learn very quickly to tell each of his parents what they want to hear in the hope that he will be saved from their fights.

Research tells us that as James gets older there is a strong chance he will lack the skills to properly express his feelings. Instead he may become defiant, withdraw from the world around him or abuse drugs and alcohol.

Just like the citizens of France and Germany that survived World War II, James may learn to cope, but will be scarred for life.

Anne and Bill are **high-conflict parents** – those parents whose relationship after separation is like that of warring nations. This form of post-separation parenting is the most damaging for both parents and children.

Signs of high-conflict parenting include:

- **They cannot agree on anything.** These parents will operate from a place where one will say the sky is blue and the other will say it is green. Neither will be able to accept that the other may be right or even just see things differently. They will not be able to agree on the simplest things for their children – daily health treatment, school activities and extra-curricular activities. Every decision to be made becomes a fight as neither parent can compromise.

- **They disagree about who will meet the financial costs of the children.** These parents will often be involved in ongoing disputes about the costs of their children and often are constantly appealing decisions that might be made by the Child Support Agency about those costs.

- **They will engage in arguments at changeover for the children and then almost daily by text and email.** The fight and who might 'win' is the focus, instead of their children.

- **They have no trust in each other.** I have seen children taken to multiple medical practitioners just because one of their parents will not believe the other when they are told that a child may be unwell. Often the child's medical treatment will suffer as the practitioners themselves may choose not to be involved or are not authorised to treat the child.
- These families are generally involved in the Court process and often keep going back over simple things regarding their children.
- Often one or both of the parents may suffer from a form of a personality disorder, making them very challenging to deal with and their rigidness often fuels much of the conflict.

Children who experience high-conflict parenting for the duration of their childhood are at significant risk of developmental harm. These children may:

- Lose their ability to trust others
- Have low self-belief
- Have little capacity to manage their own emotions
- Demonstrate their distress by acting out or through poor behaviour
- Have difficulty maintaining friendships and relationships
- Not perform as well at school as other children
- Have difficulty forming healthy adult relationships later in life

High-conflict parents will be the first to tell you that they are not at fault – it is always the other person. They will be so far involved in their own conflict that they won't be able to see the 'wood for the trees'. Only with specialised professional assistance can these parents improve their parenting techniques.

I will live in Germany and you can live in France – parallel parenting

The third style of post-separation parenting is parallel parenting. It is a place somewhere between cooperative parenting and high-conflict parenting. These parents still find it very difficult to work together but they have enough trust and respect intact to parent responsibly in their own ways. These parents don't talk to each other much, but they are capable of compromise and making decisions together for their children. Like France and Germany, these parents will each have their own set of rules in each household, but they don't undermine the rules or customs that exist in the other parent's home.

Parallel parenting is perhaps a good place to start if you are in the throes of a very difficult separation, but at all times the goal should be to cooperatively parent just as France and Germany are able to coexist in the modern world for their citizens.

ROBERT'S STORY

After separating from my wife and deciding that we ultimately saw no future in our marriage, we both knew we would need to work together in the future for the benefit of our two boys.

We decided on a collaborative approach to the divorce process. Although there had been pain in the break up, we put this aside and worked out amicably how we would share our property, the custody of our children and the finances for doing so.

Some five years on from our divorce, I talk to my ex-wife about my boys on a weekly basis, we share time together with them at their birthdays, weekend sports and the occasional meal.

This truly has done wonders for the boys and while we are not what might be deemed a traditional family, the boys don't know any different and have only shown positives, including good grades, being healthy and, most importantly, being happy as a result of the co-parenting and the great communication we have.

At times this type of arrangement can have some issues, but the outcome for my boys is well worth the effort to put any differences my ex-wife and I might have to one side and we can all live a harmonious life, with well-adjusted children who ultimately have had little impact from the divorce.

THE TRICKY DIVISION OF TIME

After your separation, the time that your children spend between your home and your partner's home can be a source of great conflict. The majority of legal disputes around children relate to this issue – how will you carve up the days in a week, the weeks in a month or the months in a year so that it is the best thing for your children?

Over the years I have seen all sorts of ways that the seven days and seven nights in a week can be divided between parents to create what is said to be the 'best' living arrangement for their children. If only there were eight days and eight nights in a week – the mathematics would be so much easier for us as adults, though it probably isn't any better for the children who experience these arrangements day in and day out.

For almost every parent, the physical time you spend with your children after a marriage breakdown will be somehow different and will mostly be less than before your divorce.

We now live in a world where 'equal time' arrangements for children have become more and more common. In 2006 there was a significant shift in how Australian law deals with parenting matters, which brought into the spotlight the concept of 'equal time'. However, in 2024 there was a sort of 'shift back' to at least to remove the suggestion that equal time was the preferred starting point for many families.

Despite the more recent changes to the Family Law Act, the concept of 'equal time' is something many parents seek after separation.

'Equal time' might mean seven nights here and seven nights there, or perhaps fourteen nights divided into some regimen of three days / four days / four days / three days – any sort of division of nights that creates a sense of 'equality'. We learn very quickly in life that equality equates with fairness, and an unequal outcome tends to be equated with a 'win' or a 'loss'.

For most parents trying to establish a post-separation parenting arrangement, there is a lot to be said for the notion of 'fairness'. Equal time can be interpreted to mean that each of the parents are equally capable of parenting their children – they are perhaps just as good as each other and hence the 'equal' involvement in their children's lives. On the other hand, the idea that a parent might have less time than the other with their own children could be interpreted to mean that this parent is somehow a 'lesser' parent – that their time with their children will be less as the other parent is somehow 'better'.

If parenting was all about the time you spend with your children then I am sure these concepts might have some truth, but it is not. Parenting – good parenting – is about so much more than 'time'.

My mum was at home with us all the time. She was the regular taxi service and gave up much of her life to ensure my brothers and I could participate in so many activities at school, after school and on weekends. To this day she selflessly provides this same level of love and care, and also now for her grandchildren. My father, however, worked hard – he regularly travelled and could not spend as much 'time' in the physical sense with us as children. It was their partnership as parents that made it all work. I never questioned their love, whether they were there or not. I did not mind my dad travelling and working hard – I have learned so much from watching him. I have also learned so much from my mum's devotion to her 24/7 job as a parent.

I feel for the parents that come to my office. I can read all over their faces the sense of loss they feel knowing that the physical time they spend with their children is about to, or has already, changed. What is important to understand is that the sense of 'time' – numbers of days or nights in my legal world – is never equated with a parent's 'value'. More or less time does not mean a better or worse parent.

I would say I had 'less time' with my dad growing up, but I would never say he was any less of a parent than my mum. In their partnership they each took on different roles and it worked. They were and are amazing parents, both bringing different skills, love and attention to each of us as children.

Beyond the idea of a parent's value, imposing equal time on your children for the sake of 'fairness' may not, in fact, be the best choice for your children.

Kids are resilient little things – that is what we are told (or perhaps tell ourselves). While I am sure kids can be resilient, I am not sure that they should be placed in living arrangements that suit their parents in the hope that their resilience will get them through.

As I assist parents in negotiating the division of weeks or months between them I often stop, close my eyes and try to imagine myself as a child of a similar age to their children. I remember what I was doing then and what the arrangement these parents are suggesting might have meant for me. And sometimes equal time may not have been the best choice.

Essentially, parenting arrangements for children decided by the Court will come back to the legal principles I listed earlier that determine what is in the 'best interests' of a child. That list is broad and it doesn't always cover off on the things that really matter to you and your family.

If possible, I prefer parents to come to an arrangement themselves. When you start to contemplate the best parenting arrangement for your children, take the time to think through these things:

- What are the ages and stages of development of each of your children? Children of different ages might need different arrangements after your separation.
- What sort of personalities do they have? Consider their maturity and temperament.
- What routines have your children been used to prior to your separation?
- What changes do you think might work for them?
- The practicalities - how far is it between where you and your spouse live (or will live)? Are there costs involved in the children travelling and how could those be best managed?
- What about extended family and friends? How can your children's relationships with others be maintained and supported?
- What childcare arrangements have your children been used to? Will these need to change?
- Do you or your children have any special needs? How might this affect the parenting arrangements?
- What about religion or cultural practices and beliefs of your family - how will they be accounted for?

This is by no means an exhaustive list of considerations and every family is different. A parenting arrangement that works perfectly for your best friend's family may not necessarily work for your family.

Additionally, the arrangements that you put in place for your children immediately after separation will likely change as your children get older. If you are not certain how your children will adapt, it is also worthwhile trialling arrangements. This will require trust, respect and communication, but if you and your spouse are able to focus on your children's needs, flexibility will have many advantages.

Most importantly, remember that you will be a parent to your children for life. While the time that you spend with them while they are young is very important, your relationship with them will last well past their childhood. Just because you may not be able to spend 'equal time' with your children now does not mean that they will see you as any less of a parent later in life.

THE KEY TO LONG-TERM RELATIONSHIPS
PAUL'S STORY

I had been married for twelve years, had three beautiful children, a very nice house which my wife and I had designed and built and I had a well-paid secure job when we decided to separate.

In our discussions around the time of our separation, we both agreed that we would split the family assets fifty-fifty. However, when our house sold my wife's solicitors froze the assets and she put in a claim for 70 per cent of the family assets and also a claim for my superannuation. At the time I was seeking to have a parenting arrangement approved by the Family Court where our youngest child would live with me and the other two with my wife and we would have access to the children on alternating weekends and one evening during the week.

The only way I was able to secure the parenting agreement was to agree to the seventy per cent asset split which I thought unfair given I would be paying child support and I needed to have accommodation to house the children when they were in my care.

However, once the finances were sorted the Parenting Plan worked well for several years.

Problems arose when my former wife decided to move approximately an hour's drive away. She disregarded the parenting agreement, which was subsequently not upheld by the Family Court. She also lured the youngest child away with her and would not agree to meet me halfway to transfer children for shared visits. I was devastated. Having been in regular contact with the children I now only saw them when I drove to visit them. These meetings might have only been for one or two hours. I had nowhere to spend time with them and they would not come and stay with me for the weekend. It didn't take long before the children said they were too busy to see me, or had other arrangements. My contact was limited to occasional phone calls and in time I would only see the children on their birthdays.

At that stage I was at my lowest. I was depressed, angry at the Court system, angry with my ex and I felt like chucking in my job so I didn't have to pay child support. What I didn't realise at the time was that I needed to focus more on the positive things happening in my life and pursue my career. At the time of my separation my career was put on hold – in hindsight, I should have put aside my concerns about child support payments and pursued my career through further study and taking on leadership roles in my organisation to improve my income.

Eventually, with the support of a new partner, I pulled myself out of my rut. Through encouragement, I maintained regular phone contact with the children. I met with them and celebrated major anniversaries and events (birthdays, Father's Day, Christmas) and I kept our conversations focused on them and what was happening in their world rather than trying to apportion blame.

As the children finished high school they moved out of their mother's home and I was able to re-establish my connection with them. I would continue visiting them and they were always welcome at my home. Now after fifteen years of separation, I have a wonderful relationship with all three of my children. My work has taken me to the city where my children now live. I see my eldest daughter weekly, my youngest has moved into my home (I'm told it's only temporary) and my son and I chat regularly and we meet up when he is not off travelling or interstate.

IS THERE A 'RIGHT WAY'?

There is no one perfect way to construct parenting arrangements for children after the breakdown of your relationship. Perhaps the main thing to keep in mind when thinking about arrangements for your children is this – children at different ages will benefit from different parenting regimes. What might work for a thirteen-year-old is unlikely to work as well for a six-month-old baby.

As a parent you will know that your children change almost every day, and the time that a mother might spend with a very young baby clearly changes as that child ages. Depending on your family unit and the roles that each of you as parents has undertaken, the arrangements for your children could vary significantly.

If your children are very young at the time of your separation, it is likely that the parenting arrangements you put in place now will change as your children get older and their needs change.

Every child is different, just as every family is different. For this reason, there is no set arrangement that you must follow and Judges with many years of experience regularly say that parents are the people best armed with the tools needed to make decisions for their children after a separation.

Here are some things to consider that might assist when you are discussing or proposing arrangements for your children:

- **What sort of parenting arrangements were your children used to during your relationship?** If your family had a stay-at-home parent and a working parent, your children may have been used to arrangements where one of you has taken on the primary parent role. It is quite common now in Australia for families to have two full-time working parents, and in those families it's often the case that children are well used to being cared for by one or both parents at different times. The arrangements that your children were used to prior to your separation can of course change after your separation, but it's important to take them into account as you formulate new arrangements. You may want to make the transition gradual for children if they are used to being cared for by one of their parents, but moving to an arrangement in which they are cared for equally by both parents.
- **Are your children very young?** Very young children tend to benefit from arrangements in which they spend most of their time with their primary attachment figure. Historically in many families this has been the mother, but in modern society this is not always the case. When I say very young children, I mean those under twenty-four months. If any of your children are very young at the time of your separation, it is worth considering having a series of short-term parenting plans or parenting agreements, rather than trying to predict the parenting arrangements for your children well into their teenage years. This way you and your former partner can test different things to see how your children cope.

- **Do you have children of different ages?** Sometimes the hardest parenting arrangements to consider are when you have children whose ages vary from very young to teenagers. It is quite common for these families to have different arrangements for each child, taking into account their unique needs. This, of course, requires cooperation between parents, but can sometimes produce much better results for the children involved. Think about the different ages of your children and whether it might be better to consider arrangements that are specific to each child. Generally it's best if siblings can travel with each other as a sibship unit, but if you have a toddler and a teenager in your family, it might be best to consider different arrangements for each of those children.
- **Do you have teenagers?** Parenting teenagers is never easy and perhaps even harder after separation. If you are dealing with children aged fifteen and above, no doubt their personal views will have a big impact on the arrangements you might consider appropriate for them. Not only their views but also their routines become incredibly important at this age. Teenagers will often be under significant pressure at school, be trying to maintain friendship groups, and on the weekend are sometimes engaged in part-time employment. Like with all children, consistency and routine remains important, but taking into account their views and wishes is essential if you want the parenting arrangements to work. This doesn't mean that just because a teenager suggests something, that it should happen. What is important is to try to understand what they consider best as part of any discussion you and your partner have about arrangements for them.

- **Consider the personalities of your children.** The personality and temperament of any child will influence how well they can cope with the change. It is, of course, not uncommon with multiple children in a family to have very different personalities or temperaments among the siblings. While this cannot always be balanced perfectly, it's something that should be considered by you and your spouse when you are discussing parenting arrangements. If you have a child that is particularly attached to one parent, it might be important to work at building the attachment with the other parent rather than simply encouraging the already secure attachment with the first parent. You might have children who are very robust or children who are very shy and vulnerable. Again, if you are considering changing the routines or arrangements that they've been used to for some time, it's worth considering how you think the personalities or temperaments of your children may or may not be affected by any change.
- **Do your children have any unique needs?** Specific health needs can affect your parenting arrangements. Depending on the significance of any health needs, if a parent has not been used to dealing with those needs, it might be best to consider whether you, as parents, can share information to make things easier for your children. This is particularly true for any children with special needs. If you have a special needs child, you will no doubt have much knowledge about what is best for your child and you should take that medical opinion and advice into account when you are considering the parenting arrangements for your children, and that child in particular, moving forward.

Remember there is no one right way to divide the time your children spend between you and your partner after your separation. Think carefully about your own family, your children and your routines and don't be afraid to try different things to see what works best.

WHAT DO YOUR KIDS NEED FROM YOU?

While the law sets out a series of important principles that might be considered when making arrangements for children, as parents there are simple things you can do to support your children through your separation.

Keep the following dos and don'ts in mind to help your children cope with your separation:

1. **Do try to cooperate with your partner.** Remember that both of you will always be parents and, to be able to parent effectively, you will need to cooperate. Unlike when you were in an intact relationship, your new relationship as parents will have significant boundaries. For example, neither of you will be able to control what the other is doing in their time with your children. Your capacity to cooperate for the benefit of your children while understanding the new boundaries around your relationship as parents is essential to ensuring that your children are protected from the negative impacts of separation, and have the best chance to develop into successful adults.
2. **Do set a good example.** Children model and learn their behaviours from significant adults in their lives, particularly their parents. Your behaviours in dealing with conflict, sadness, loss, happiness and success will be learned by your children and may play out in their relationships in future. By sheltering

your children from conflict, protecting them from the adult issues that surround your relationship breakdown and reassuring them they are loved, you will help teach them how to have healthy relationships in future.

3. **Don't believe everything they tell you.** Children always should be sheltered and protected from any arguments and disputes between you and your former partner. Don't require your children to make decisions about things such as the time they will spend with you or their other parent or other significant people in their lives. Children will feel torn and will often tell you things that they think you will want to hear to try to make you happy. Children often behave this way to try to show their love for you. However, like saying that they're sick to get out of going to school, what they say isn't always reliable. The difference is that, once your relationship has ended, the level of communication between you and your partner will have reduced. At this time, a parent can be somewhat suspicious or watch the children closely to quickly observe any negative impacts of separation. Now, instead of saying, 'I don't want to go to school,' the child is saying, 'I don't want to go to Mummy's house.' All of a sudden the enquiry becomes quite long-winded, detailed and draining for both the child and the parent.

4. **Do be consistent.** It is important that you as parents try to be consistent and have a mutual approach to issues concerning your children. A high level of communication between the two of you does not mean that you need to talk every day, but rather that when you do talk, email or meet, you make the most of those situations and try to agree on ways to deal with the hurdles that come up from time to time. For example, speaking about how you would manage a conversation with your child who says they don't want to

go to your home or the other parent's home can ensure that both of you are presenting your children with consistency and creating the security and boundaries that they need to grow and develop.

5. **Do provide a consistent routine.** Children with consistent routines have the best chance of feeling a sense of security, enabling them to enjoy all the benefits of being a child. For example, consistency across two households in the bedtime and sleep routine of very young children will minimise stress and sleep issues for the child. If your child has a special toy or comfort item, let them take it with them to both households. Children's personal belongings, particularly toys and the like, should be able to travel freely between the two homes. This may mean that, from time to time, things leave your home and don't come back, but it is important that children enjoy their things no matter where they are. Sometimes it can be helpful to have more than one if it's a particular toy or blanket. That way, if it is ever forgotten in one person's home, there is always a back-up. For older children, it is important that there are similar routines for things such as schoolwork and extra-curricular activities. There is nothing more obstructive for children and their peers if your child is the one that can only go to every second soccer game because their parents couldn't agree on their son or daughter participating in soccer in the first place. Your households do not need to be the same, nor do your parenting styles, but consistency with routines will promote security and reassure your children. Remember France and Germany – different cultures, customs and cuisines, but I can happily move between the two nations every day if I please because of the understanding and respect that is in place.

6. **Never communicate through your children.** Using your children to deliver messages, no matter how unimportant, will make them party to the dispute between you and your partner. Children should not be burdened with tasks that their parents should be undertaking. Communication is the key to a good post-separation parenting relationship and, as difficult as it may be to communicate with your former partner, it is essential that you find an effective way of doing this. To achieve this it is important that you give some thought to the style, frequency and communication process that you and your spouse can best use, keeping in mind that your type and style of communication may change over time. Immediately after separation, there is normally a high level of mistrust, emotion, hurt and anger. Perhaps you and your partner might initially retreat to written communication as a way of ensuring that you can slow down and think about what each of you is saying. Over time, you might consider including telephone calls to update each other as to how the children are progressing. Try to be open in your communication and don't withhold information that relates to your children.

7. **Don't question your children about the time they are spending with your former spouse.** I enjoy coming home at the end of the day and asking my daughter what she has done that day. Today when I asked her that question, she told me that she'd been to the beach. She hadn't been to the beach, in fact she hadn't been there for some weeks now but that was what flowed off her tongue. Similarly, I enjoy speaking with my five-year-old nephew on the phone from time to time. When I ask him what he has been doing today, I will get a clearer answer from him than from my young daughter, but often

what he has done over the last week flows into the conversation. Children do not have the same concepts of time that we as adults do. Nor do they have the same concepts of experiences. While you might think that the information you are receiving from your children is accurate, it may not be, and it is important not to make them feel they are being questioned in depth about what they have been doing because, before you know it, they will start either adding information or telling you what they think you want to hear. Allow them to share their experiences with you, and if you need any reassurance, consider asking your former partner to clarify their comments. Sometimes a changeover is the perfect opportunity to ask your former spouse what the kids have been doing so that you can share those experiences with them. For example, if the children have been to a special concert, family event or holiday, it can be nice to at least know that it has occurred. This way you can have conversations where you are reassuring your children that the experiences they are having, both in your home and outside your home, are equally important to you and to them.

8. **Don't impose unnecessary restrictions.** I am commonly asked by my clients, who are not experiencing some level of fear or danger, whether they need to disclose where they are now living. I answer that question by asking that parent whether they would feel comfortable not knowing where their children are when they are not with them. In my experience, most parents would like to know where their children are most of the time, more for peace of mind than anything else. Always remember that if you impose restrictions or require commitments from your former partner, those are likely to flow both

ways. Always stop and think to yourself whether a piece of information that you are considering withholding is something that you would want to know about if the ball was in the other court.

9. **Do focus on yourself (not your former partner).** Traditional legal processes, particularly the Court process, will by their very nature force you to focus on your former partner, particularly on any of their wrongdoings. While you cannot change the actions of your former partner, you can change your own actions and reactions. Focus your attention on what you are doing in any given situation and whether there is a better way that you could approach it. As the saying goes, 'There are many ways to skin a cat.' Not a particularly pleasant saying, but the concept is correct. There may be times when you feel boxed into a corner and with very few options. However, we always have choices in life, particularly as to how we act in any given situation. Sometimes stepping away from the situation and taking the time to consider how we could act or react differently can be enough to change a situation. If you can focus your attention on what you are doing, rather than what your former spouse is doing wrong, this will help you to move through this difficult period more quickly. It is also likely that you did not always agree on parenting techniques when you were together. It is probably not surprising that this will continue after your separation.

10. **Do focus on the good (not the bad).** It is so easy to find things that are wrong in any given situation and yet at times so difficult to find the things that are right. When you feel that things are becoming really tough, stop, take a pause, and think about two things that are going right. They might be simple things like your son or daughter receiving a good school report or doing well in an activity or reaching a new milestone. It is important to always remind yourself of the small successes among what you sometimes feel are many failures. If you can turn your mind to the positives and the things that are going right, the things that you may have thought were going wrong will start to pale in significance.

11. **Do be flexible.** Parenting in an intact, happy relationship is hard work. Every day parents are shifting their own lives to ensure their children are given every opportunity to pursue their dreams and live their lives to the fullest. You have to be flexible as a parent, as things often seem to go slightly off course when kids are involved. Nothing will change after your separation, other than it is perhaps more difficult to manage the unexpected. Don't be afraid to be flexible and show understanding if your partner asks for variations to your parenting arrangements. You will no doubt need the same in return one day. Of course if this starts to happen every Friday night, it might be time to meet and discuss whether the arrangements are still working for your family.

If you and your partner can do these things, regardless of the legal process and their new living arrangements, your children are unlikely to be emotionally affected by your divorce and separation.

He taught me housekeeping; when I divorce I keep the house.

ZSA ZSA GABOR

Show me the money!

THE SECOND LEGAL ISSUE

After parenting arrangements, the second legal area that you will encounter after your separation is the division of your finances and assets.

When it comes to money, assets, debts, income and the 'stuff' (as I like to call it) that you each own, there are three main areas to be aware of:

1. **Property settlement.** This is the division of what the law considers to be your 'property'. In a simplistic sense this is pretty much anything you own that has value (even the kitchen sink!).

2. **Spouse maintenance.** This is the term that relates to the financial support that might be paid by one spouse to the other when that spouse is unable to otherwise adequately support themselves. Spouse maintenance is similar to the American concept of alimony. It is usually in the form of a weekly or

monthly amount but can also include the transfer of assets or lump sum amounts.

3. **Child support.** This is the payment made by one parent to another to assist with the costs of raising children. Child support is usually paid until children are eighteen years of age and is generally administered by the Department of Human Services.

In this chapter, I will cover these three areas in detail.

I JUST WANT THE HOUSE! PROPERTY SETTLEMENTS AND THE FAMILY LAW

The division of your assets, liabilities, superannuation and pretty much anything else with any value after your separation is known as your 'property settlement'. A property settlement can be done at any time after separation and, in the case of married couples, you do not have to wait until you are divorced.

There are, however, some important time limitations that relate to property settlement matters. If you are married, you have until twelve months from the date of your divorce to have either finalised your property settlement or to have at least filed an application in the appropriate Family Court seeking Orders for property division. Alternatively, if you are in a de facto relationship, you have only two years from the date of your final separation to formalise your property division or bring the necessary application. If you are outside of these time limitations, it is important that you seek legal advice immediately, as this can have a significant impact on your legal rights and entitlements.

When it comes to assessing how assets, liabilities and superannuation should be divided between married and de facto couples, there is a four-step process.[4] The law in relation to both married and de facto relationships, as far as the division of assets and the like are concerned, is almost identical in most states of Australia.[5]

Step 1: What assets, liabilities and superannuation do you have?

The Court must first determine what assets, liabilities and financial resources are to be considered in determining the property division.

In essence a list of everything that you and your partner own is created. It does not matter if your home is registered in your name, your partner's name or even a friend's name. If you own it (or part of it), it will go on the list. This is also the case for debts and other liabilities.

---

4 For the specific legislation relating to property settlements for married couples you should consider Part VIII of the Family Law Act (Cth) 1974 and for Defacto relationships, Part VIIIAB. Superannuation matters are dealt with generally in Part VIIIB of the Act. Some case law has suggested that there may in fact be a '5 stage process' but for the purposes of this book I have not touched on that more complicated legal step and it would be appropriate to ensure you obtain advice specific to your circumstances.

5 The legislation and operation of the Family Courts in WA is slightly different to that in states around Australia. The effect of that legislation though is largely the same as the Family Law Act (Cth). You should get advice from a Family Lawyer specific to your circumstances.

It is the value of those assets now that is the starting point. Even if you separated five years ago, it will still be the value of the items you hold now that is of immediate relevance. Generally, we undertake this step by writing a list, often in a table, of everything that you have – like in the following example.

ASSETS			
ITEM	**VALUE**	**OWNERSHIP**	**NOTES**
Home	$800,000	Joint	Held as joint tenants. Value is estimated – to be agreed or valued.
Savings account	$5,500	Joint	Used as working account to meet living expenses.
Car (Toyota)	$20,000	Wife	Value is estimated from RedBook.
Car (Holden)	$25,000	Husband	Value is estimated from RedBook.
Shares	$35,000	Husband	Value is estimated from ASX, to be confirmed closer to settlement date.
TOTAL	**$885,000**		

LIABILITIES			
ITEM	**VALUE**	**OWNERSHIP**	**NOTES**
Home mortgage	($210,000)	Joint	In joint names.
Credit card	($3,500)	Husband	Both parties have access to credit card.
TOTAL	**($213,500)**		

SUPERANNUATION			
ITEM	**VALUE**	**OWNERSHIP**	**NOTES**
QSuper	$540,000	Husband	Value from last super statement - to be updated.
SunSuper	$415,000	Wife	Value current.
TOTAL	**$955,000**		
TOTAL POOL	**$2,627,000**		

Things to keep in mind regarding this asset pool:

- **Home contents.** You will see I have not included a reference to home contents and other personal belongings in the table above. When it comes to valuing these items, it is the second-hand (or sale) value of the furniture and other personal items that you own that is important, not the insured value. There is often a very significant difference between those two numbers. The last time I had a client value all the items in their home, the valuer concluded that the contents of a standard four-bedroom home were worth somewhere between $6,000 and $7,000. Those contents, however, were insured for well over $100,000. To save yourself time and money, I would strongly recommend that you and your spouse try to agree on the division of your personal items and home contents. It will often be cheaper to buy new furniture items than to argue, through solicitors or any other legal process, over the division of those items.

- **Motor vehicles.** In legal practice we often use the websites 'Redbook' or 'Carsales' to gauge an estimated value for motor vehicles. You can do this yourself very easily, as long as you have information about the car, including the model, make, year and kilometres it has driven. RedBook is a good guide at this stage to give you an estimate of the value of vehicles at a low cost. It is not evidence, however, and a formal valuation may later be needed if you find yourself before a Court.
- **Homes and other real estate.** If you and your spouse cannot agree on an estimated value for your home or any other real estate that you own, you can obtain appraisals from real estate agents or a formal valuation. If you choose to obtain appraisals, make sure you explain to the agents what the appraisal is for. In my experience, you can obtain quite varied appraisals on homes from real estate agents and sometimes it is more beneficial to obtain a valuation early in the piece. A valuation should be obtained from a registered valuer and will often cost between $1,000 and $2,000 per property. A valuer will provide you with a written report, including comparable sales in your area and their expert view on the appropriate sale price of the property in question. If you have commercial properties, it is important to also consider the market rent that can be received for those properties, as this can heavily affect their value.
- **Superannuation.** Superannuation is one of the easier assets to value. There are different types of superannuation interests, ranging from 'accumulation interests' (think of them like a savings account that just keeps accruing with your regular contributions) to 'defined benefit interests' (often associated

with public service funds, which are difficult to value as they depend on the length of service and final salary payable). A lot of families now have self-managed superannuation funds, which are different again.

Depending on the type of superannuation benefit or interest that you hold, you may need to obtain different valuation information. You should speak to your fund or fund manager about the type of interest you hold and how best to obtain valuation information. Under the Family Law Act, you can issue a document called a 'Form 6' (see the Family Law Courts website, www.fcfcoa.gov.au) to either your fund or your spouse's fund to obtain an up-to-date valuation or even a historical valuation of your or your spouse's superannuation interest.

The process of identifying all your assets, liabilities and superannuation can be simple or onerous. If businesses are involved, it is important to obtain independent and expert advice on their value. You can assist your legal and other professional advisers by at least compiling a list of what you think you have and providing an estimate of what you think the values might be. The more you and your spouse can agree upon regarding value, the simpler the process will be. It is, however, important to consider obtaining valuation advice and expertise where necessary. Your professional advisers, including your lawyers, are likely to ask for supporting documentation to assist them in undertaking this process of identifying the assets that you hold. For example, copies of recent bank statements, mortgage accounts, credit card statements and the like will often be required to help with this identification process. Again, you can assist your legal advisers by gathering any required documents that are requested in a timely fashion.

Step 2: How did you create the wealth that you have?

The second phase of the legal process for your property division is to consider how you and your partner together created the assets, liabilities, superannuation and other financial resources that you now have. In the legal framework you will hear this called 'contributions'.

There are generally three main types of contributions:

- First, those from income or other financial sources called, of course, **financial contributions**, which may include gifts, inheritances and other large lump sums.
- Second, **non-financial contributions**, such as unpaid work in a family business or an owner builder undertaking renovations to real estate.
- Third, **contributions to the welfare of the family**, such as the day-to-day running of the household and care of children.
    - At this stage the legal process will also consider:
    - The impact of family violence during a relationship on the contributions made by each party.
    - The effect of any proposed Order on the income-earning capacity of a party.
    - Any child support paid / received for a child of the relationship.

Each relationship is made up of very different contributions, and it is for this reason that the Court will look at each relationship on its own facts. There is no hard and fast rule, it is a balancing of the different contributions in your relationship.

It's also important at this stage of the four-step process to consider the timing of any contributions. We look here to contributions that were made at the outset of your relationship, often called 'initial contributions'. For example, if either of you had significant assets or debts at the beginning of your relationship, this may have an impact on how your property settlement is calculated now.

We then look at the contributions that were made during your relationship and then finally we might look at the period after your separation, often called 'post-separation contributions'. If it has been a long time since your separation, contributions made after the breakdown of your relationship can become relevant in the assessment of your property division.

There's a lot of information that your family lawyer will need to glean to be able to accurately balance and assess the contributions that you and your partner have made to the 'conservation, improvement and acquisition' of any of the property of your relationship. Additionally, every family and every relationship is different and how you have created or contributed to the wealth you have will be different from any other family. There is also no starting position or assumption that things will be divided equally.

It is, therefore, essential that you obtain advice specific to your circumstances from an experienced family lawyer.

Step 3: Which other factors must be considered in your circumstances?

The third stage of your property settlement assessment is to consider a variety of factors that are set out in the Family Law Act.[6] I call this the 'crystal ball' step.

At this third stage of the process, we are trying to look into a crystal ball and predict the financial future of both you and your spouse, using the information from your past to ultimately predict your future. Therefore, the things that are relevant at this stage of the consideration include:

- **Family violence.** Whether there has been family violence and how it has affected the other person's circumstances.
- **Age and health.** The age and state of health of each person.
- **Financial position.** Each person's income, property, financial resources, and ability to earn an income in the future.
- **Wastage of assets.** Whether either person has recklessly or deliberately wasted money or property.
- **Debts or liabilities.** The debts of each person, and the nature and circumstances of those debts.
- **Caring for children.** Who has the primary care of children under eighteen, and the need to provide housing for them.
- **Living commitments.** Each person's commitments to support themselves, their children or other dependants.
- **Support obligations.** Any legal duty to financially support another person (for example, a dependent family member).

---

6 See section 79(5) for married couples or section 90SM(5) for Defacto couples of the Family Law Act 1975 (Cth) for the full list of factors to be considered.

- **Pensions and benefits.** Whether either person is eligible for government benefits, pensions or superannuation entitlements.
- **Standard of living.** The reasonable standard of living for each person after separation.
- **Future opportunities.** Whether adjusting property interests would help one person study, start a business or earn an adequate income.
- **Impact on creditors.** Whether a proposed Order would affect the ability of creditors to recover debts.
- **Contributions to the other person.** Whether one person has contributed to the other's income, career or financial resources.
- **Length of the marriage.** How long the marriage lasted and how it affected each person's career or earning capacity.
- **Parenting role.** The need to protect a person's ability to continue caring for children.
- **New relationships.** If either person is living with someone else, the financial impact of that new relationship.

Just as the assessment of contributions in Step 2 is complicated, Step 3 is similarly complicated and discretionary. Chances are, if you take your circumstances to three or four different family lawyers, you will end up with three or four different answers! All of those answers are likely to be 'right', as far as the law is concerned, making this one of the most challenging parts of being a family lawyer and, no doubt, one of the most difficult parts for separating families to grapple with!

Step 4: Is the overall division appropriate?

After identifying the assets, balancing contributions and then considering the further relevant factors in your case, this fourth step is an assessment to ensure that the outcome is 'just and equitable'. Importantly, the law does not refer to the word 'fair'.

You will hear family lawyers or Courts talking about the overall division of the property pool of two people in percentage terms. There is no precise science to reaching a decision, as every relationship is different, but a Court must ultimately be satisfied that a division is just and equitable, or appropriate, at law.

What else to keep in mind for your property division

You are probably more confused than ever about the application of these four steps to your circumstances. This is an area where you need to seek specialist advice. There is no magic book that sets out the likely outcome based on the years of your relationship or the value of your property. There are a few things you should always keep in mind:

- **Contributions as a stay-at-home parent in longer relationships are equal to or just as valuable as contributions made by a working person.** It does not matter if the stay-at-home person is a terrible cook or if the working person is a high-income earner – as a general rule, it is accepted in relationships that we each take on different roles and these roles are all as valuable as each other.

- **Superannuation can be divided between you.** It is possible to move superannuation between the two of you – this does not mean that you can access it earlier than you would otherwise be able to; it means that your or your partner's superannuation can be moved to the other's superannuation account. This is particularly useful in families where one party has primarily stayed at home and has limited superannuation. While you may not be so interested in superannuation now, chances are you might be grateful you considered it once you move into retirement.
- **'All women end up with seventy per cent.'** I hear a lot from clients that women will always get about seventy to eighty per cent of the asset pool after separation. This is entirely incorrect. There is no 'usual thing' when it comes to property settlements, just like there is no 'usual family financial situation. Every outcome will be different.
- **No marriage or de facto relationship is the same.** Building on the previous point, remember that every case and every family is different. I often see clients who tell me that, when speaking with friends or family, they heard that they should receive a certain percentage share or outcome in their property settlement because that was what their friend had received and their circumstances were very similar. However, there are so many different variables that affect a property settlement that it is very rare that the outcome in two separate relationships or two different families will be the same. Things like the length of the relationship, contributions that were made to it, the type of assets that are available for division and the financial future of the parties involved can create very different outcomes in similar circumstances.

- **The law is discretionary in this area.** Unlike in personal injury law or some commercial disputes, when it comes to Family Law matters, including property division, the law has a discretionary element. This means that your same circumstances could be placed before four or five different Judges and four or five different results would ensue. All of those results would be appropriate at law. In our profession we often talk of there being somewhere around a ten per cent differential that captures all the correct outcomes in a property settlement. This means that one Judge might award you, say, forty per cent of your overall asset pool, while another might award you fifty per cent. Both outcomes, and any number in the middle, would still be correct at law. It is this discretionary element that can make it quite difficult for lawyers to provide specific advice on this area. As such, you will find that your lawyer is likely to advise you on your property division by considering a range of outcomes, from your best-case to your worst-case outcome. In any settlement discussions it is unlikely that you will receive your best-case scenario. You should also consider that to achieve a 'best-case' scenario, you would need to factor in the financial and time cost of pursuing a matter in court, along with the emotional cost to you, your family and your friends.
- **Balance in commercial realities.** It's important to focus on the value of the settlement and the impact certain assets may have on your life going forward, rather than focusing on a certain percentage of the pool. In my experience, it can be common for couples in property settlement matters to become quite fixated on achieving a particular percentage outcome. For

example, if you are told early in your matter that you will achieve something like a seventy per cent outcome, it is unlikely that you will then want to settle for a sixty per cent share of the assets that you hold. The difficulty is, however, that to achieve your seventy per cent outcome you may need to pursue your matter through litigation or the Court process. This will take significant time - generally more than a year and a half - before you appear before a Judge for a trial. The Court process is very expensive, and over that year and a half you will spend a significant amount of money on legal fees (usually at least $150,000 for you and a similar amount for your former spouse). This expense then cuts into your combined asset pool, meaning there is less that can be divided in the end.

For example, if you and your partner's assets are worth $1 million dollars and you together spend $300,000 on legal fees, you have spent thirty per cent of your asset pool. In those circumstances, you could argue it would have been better for you to have accepted a proposal that was a sixty per cent share of the asset pool, enabling you to invest your monies, have financial security and move forward, rather than spending the extra ten per cent you wanted to gain on legal fees.

You should also factor in the emotional costs of a Court proceeding on you and your family, as well as the personal impact, particularly in terms of time away from work and the sense that, financially, you won't be able to move forward until those proceedings are finalised.

When receiving advice in relation to property settlement matters, always ask your lawyer to break down for you the costs involved in proceeding in a litigious or Court dispute, including the financial costs, the estimated time and the likely impact on the assets that you will receive.

ROGER'S STORY

I was recently acting for a forty-five-year-old man named Roger. He and his wife Sandra separated and were negotiating their property division. Roger was still paying for the mortgage for the former marital home, which was costing him around $2,000 a month. Sandra was living in the home, so Roger had had to obtain alternate rental accommodation.

Roger and Sandra had limited equity in their home, but Sandra was hoping to keep it as a part of any property division. Roger agreed to Sandra keeping the home, but wanted to receive a cash payment to account for his share of the equity. The cash payment he hoped to receive was only between $10,000 and $20,000.

When discussing a proposal for settlement, I spoke to Roger about the impact on him on continuing to pay the mortgage for, say, another twelve months if he and Sandra were unable to reach an agreement. Twelve months of the mortgage would add up to $24,000, while the settlement that Roger hoped to receive was less than that amount.

In those circumstances, it was more beneficial for Roger to reach a settlement immediately and receive a smaller cash payment, or even no payment at all, rather than pursuing lengthy settlement discussions, or even litigation, with Sandra if it meant he would have to pay the mortgage in the intervening period.

- **The 'value' of the type of assets that you might receive in your final division.** The type of assets, liabilities and superannuation that you receive can have a significant impact on your capacity in the future to financially rebuild your life and look after your family, so take the time to get financial advice about how you can best structure your financial settlement to meet your needs. If you are thirty-eight years of age there is little point in taking a settlement that includes only a large superannuation component when there might be other assets available, such as cash or property. Look past the percentage division and instead focus on the true value of an asset to you. For example, a negatively geared and highly encumbered investment home may have an equity value that is very small, but if you have a high income that property may offer some taxation benefits that won't necessarily be reflected in your asset division. Also, if that property is in an area that you believe will improve in value over time, you might also consider the future value of that investment to you. When it comes to your property division, the value of individual assets to you will often be far more than the dollar figure that is represented on the page. This is why I encourage you to consider the impact of the type of assets you are receiving, rather than focusing on achieving a large percentage share.

PAM'S STORY

I assisted Pam with her property settlement. Pam was fifty-two and had been out of the workforce for most of her marriage after having children. Her marriage had lasted almost twenty-five years. She had just started working one day a week when I met with her.

She and her husband had accrued between them wealth that consisted of a series of properties and a large superannuation fund. Pam and I spent some time talking about her financial future and her goals. She liked living in her beautiful home in an exclusive Brisbane suburb – she had lived there for close to twenty years, the children still returned at Christmas and her friends and social circles were all close by.

The problem was that Pam did not have much of an income and the house made up over half of Pam's and Bob's property pool. For Pam to retain the home as a part of their property settlement, she would in essence receive no other assets. This would make it difficult for her to meet the ongoing costs of the home including rates, insurances, maintenance and other day-to-day living expenses, and would also affect any amount of income that Bob might be required to pay her by way of spousal maintenance.

At this point, Pam and I spent some time looking at alternative options. For example, Pam agreed that Bob could keep the main home and she would receive the smaller home (currently used as an investment property) that they owned, plus a sum of cash and perhaps, even, a superannuation split. Another option was for Pam and Bob to sell their home and each divide the proceeds, and split their remaining assets between them.

The financial adviser that Pam consulted was able to show her on paper the impact of each of those options on her financial circumstances over the next five years and beyond. By downsizing to a smaller home in the same area, she would be able to have a much more comfortable lifestyle that would enable her to continue to travel overseas each year, and would not require her to return to the workforce in any onerous way.

Each of those outcomes provided the same percentage division of her and Bob's assets on paper, but in dollar terms, each of the outcomes meant a very different financial future for Pam.

Having considered all of this, please keep in mind that I cannot tell you without having met with you, gathered lots of information, understood your goals and values and more about your family, what the likely outcome of your property settlement might be. So please do take the time to meet with a specialist family lawyer to ensure that you receive advice tailored to your circumstances.

DO I NEED TO PAY THEM MONEY AFTER OUR SEPARATION? SPOUSE MAINTENANCE

Aside from your property division, there is sometimes a need for one partner to provide financial support to the other. This occurs when one party is unable to financially support themselves.

Spouse maintenance can take different forms, including:

- **Periodic cash payments.** For example, $250 a week or $2,000 a month;
- **Payments in kind.** Meaning the payment of expenses on behalf of a partner, including mortgage payments, utility bills and other regular fixed expenses; and
- **Lump sum payments.** These are intended to meet a partner's regular living expenses, for example a $10,000 payment to enable a partner to meet their living expenses for a period of time.

Spouse maintenance is generally paid for a short and fixed period. It is not intended to be a payment that lasts forever, but it is assessed on a case-by-case basis. Often spouse maintenance is paid immediately after a separation until the property settlement is affected. Sometimes it is paid for a few years after the separation to assist a spouse with caring for children or to allow them time to be able to financially support themselves while they re-enter the paid workforce.

Over my career I have seen a steady decrease in the number of spousal maintenance arrangements for separated couples. This seems to be for two main reasons:

- First, social changes have meant that a lot more women are now in the workforce (both part time and full time) than ever before, and
- Second, there seems to be a general dislike of the idea of 'paying' your ex-partner in weekly or monthly amounts. I have noticed a similar dislike from people who may be entitled to receive spousal maintenance. As such, more couples are choosing options in which the person entitled to receive spousal maintenance receives a larger share of the property division or some other form of lump sum amount so that the financial ties between them as a couple are severed.

The legal test for spousal maintenance

Not everyone will be required to make spouse maintenance payments or be eligible to receive them. To determine whether a person is eligible to receive a form of spousal maintenance, there are in essence two enquiries that will be made:

First, does that person have a need for spousal maintenance? To assess 'need', the actual and necessary weekly expenses of the person claiming spouse maintenance are tallied. That amount is then subtracted from their income. If their necessary expenses outweigh their income, that person can demonstrate a 'need' for spousal maintenance.

RUTH'S STORY

Ruth is fifty-five and works two days a week, earning $750 after tax. She is required to pay the following weekly expenses:

ITEM	AMOUNT
Rent	$500
Groceries and other necessities	$250
Petrol	$50
Car registration / maintenance	$20
Clothing and other personal items	$100
Utilities, phone, internet	$60
TOTAL	**$980**

Therefore, to determine if Ruth might be eligible for some financial support, you would subtract Ruth's expenses from her income:

ITEM	AMOUNT
Ruth's income	$750
Less: Ruth's expenses	$980
LEAVES	**($230)**

So, Ruth needs an additional $230 a week to be able to meet her necessary expenditure.

If Ruth were in receipt of a government pension, this would obviously increase her income. However, for the purposes of establishing whether she is eligible to claim spousal maintenance, the pension amount is disregarded.

Second, can the other spouse meet that need? If one partner has established that they have a 'need' to receive spousal maintenance, the second enquiry is to assess whether the other partner has a capacity to meet that need. A similar exercise to the one above is then undertaken, considering the income of the paying spouse and subtracting their necessary expenses. If there are funds available at the end of this equation, it is likely that spousal maintenance will be paid.

RUTH'S HUSBAND – JOHN

Now let's look at Ruth's husband, John, who has a regular weekly income of $1,450. He has the following necessary expenses:

ITEM	AMOUNT
Home mortgage	$600
Groceries and other necessities	$150
Petrol	$60
Car registration / maintenance	$20
Clothing and other personal items	$40
Car finance repayment	$70
Utilities, phone, internet	$60
TOTAL	**$1,000**

Therefore, to determine if John might be capable of assisting Ruth with spousal maintenance payments:

ITEM	AMOUNT
John's income	$1,450
Less: John's expenses	$1,000
LEAVES	**$430**

John would be able to assist Ruth with spousal maintenance payments as he has $450 a week available.

In this scenario it is possible that John would be required to assist Ruth with the payment of spousal maintenance, certainly in the short term until their property settlement is resolved.

However, there might be a range of other options available to Ruth and John, for example:

- There may be savings in a joint account that could be released to Ruth to assist her in meeting her expenses.
- John might agree to Ruth moving into the home to save her rent expense, negating her need for spousal maintenance.
- Ruth might be able to increase her income by increasing her work hours.
- Ruth and John might have other assets available to them that they could use to meet Ruth's needs in the short term.

The above example is an abbreviated version intended to illustrate the process and, of course, does not include all the necessary expenses that may be associated with modern life. The assessment of what is a 'necessary expense' can be a legal battle in itself. I once had the joy of seeing a matter involving an argument around whether daily bottles of Moet were a 'necessary expense'! (It was determined that they were not.)

Spousal maintenance is a complicated area of Family Law. Do obtain advice specific to your circumstances. There are many advantages in receiving (and sometimes even paying) spousal maintenance. There can, of course, be some disadvantages and it is important to consider spousal maintenance as a part of your overall financial circumstances, including your property settlement.

CHILD SUPPORT: MANAGING THE COSTS OF CHILDREN AFTER SEPARATION

Parents have a legal obligation to maintain their children. In Australia, Services Australia manages the assessment and payment of child support by parents after separation. Previously this agency was known as the 'Child Support Agency' and you will often hear people continue to refer to it that way.

The payment of Child Support for all separated parents in Australia is determined through the application of the Child Support Act. This piece of legislation sets out a complicated formula for determining the amount of child support that should be paid by one parent to another to assist with the costs of raising their children after separation.

The formula takes into account a number of different factors, including the number of children in your family, their ages, your incomes and how much time your children spend between you and your partner.

After separation either you or your partner can make an application through Services Australia for an assessment of child support. It is not required that you do this and you are also free to make your own arrangements outside the agency.

There tend to be three main ways couples resolve their child support matters:

1. **No formal arrangement.** Many separated parents have no formal arrangements in place for child support; they might agree on an amount that will be paid by one parent to the other or they might agree to each be responsible for particular expenses. Sometimes these parents obtain an 'assessment' of child support to use as a guide but don't require the assistance of Services Australia to collect or organise those payments. Often these parents have no involvement with Services Australia and simply make their own private arrangements informally.

2. **A child support assessment.** The majority of separated parents seek assistance from Services Australia to both assess the amount of child support that is to be paid and to ensure that those amounts are paid. Some families will opt for a 'Private Collect' arrangement, meaning one partner pays directly to the other while other families will opt for an 'Agency Collect' arrangement where Services Australia will collect payments on their behalf.

3. **A child support agreement.** This is a formal contract between you and your spouse that details the terms of your child support arrangements. These agreements are often used by parents who wish to have child support arrangements that are different from those that might arise as a result of a child support assessment. For example, if your children attend private schools, or have special talents or needs, then often these expenses are not captured by the regular child support assessment. Child Support Agreements offer a lot of flexibility to parents who wish to tailor their child support arrangements to suit their family.

How is child support calculated?

Child support is a very complicated and specialised legal area. To understand the complicated formula that is used to calculate a child support assessment seems to require a PhD in 'fancy' maths. To make life easier, there is a reasonably accurate child support calculator available on the Child Support section of the Services Australia webpage (www.servicesaustralia.gov.au).

The formula considers a number of different factors, including the number of children in your family, their ages, your and your partner's incomes and how much time the children spend between you. There are many other elements to the formula that are then balanced to determine the amount of child support to be paid on a weekly basis. Once this assessment has issued, there are limited avenues to challenge or review it and you should seek specific advice from a family lawyer or the Department if you think the assessment is not accurately reflecting your family's circumstances.

Keep in mind that a child support assessment will never cover all the costs of raising children. It is also important to remember that when your children are in your care it is expected that you will be responsible for the costs associated with providing for them – clothing, food, activities and more. Paying child support does not mean that you don't contribute to the costs of your children when they are in your care.

I have seen no end of conflict between parents about who will meet the costs of an activity that a child is participating in, or perhaps meet the cost of medical or dental procedures. These expenses are for your children, so focus on that rather than getting tied up in who is paying for what. If you end up in conflict over these issues and engage lawyers, chances are it will cost more to pay your lawyer's fees than it would have to meet the cost of the expense.

If there was one final piece of advice I could leave you with regarding your property settlement, spousal maintenance and child support, it would be to focus on a quick resolution. Getting fixated on a certain percentage or dollar amount can often cause the legal process to drag on for much longer than it needs to, at a significant financial and emotional cost to you both. Instead, focus on the future and moving on as cleanly as possible.

Some people
come in your life
as blessings.
Some come in
your life
as lessons.

MOTHER TERESA

Now it's time for a divorce

THE THIRD LEGAL ISSUE

If you were married, the third legal issue to attend to is your divorce, or the dissolution of your marriage.

If you were married, you can apply for a divorce, or the dissolution of your marriage, once you have been separated for twelve months.

The process of obtaining a divorce is now one of the easiest legal steps and is something that you and your partner should be able to do without the assistance of legal advisers, if you wish. However, while a divorce will bring about a legal end to your marriage, it is important to keep in mind that it will not finalise your property division or formalise arrangements for your children.

HOW TO APPLY FOR YOUR DIVORCE

1. Visit the Family Law Courts website and download their online kit (www.fcfcoa.gov.au/fl/divorce/apply), which outlines the process and other useful information concerning your divorce.
2. Complete the Application for Divorce form, which is contained in the online kit. You can apply either with your partner or individually.
3. Sign the application before a lawyer, Justice of the Peace, or other person authorised to witness affidavits.
4. File the application with a Family Law registry, online through the Commonwealth Courts online portal (www.comcourts.gov.au).
5. If you have applied solely for the divorce, then you will need to serve the application on your spouse. There is more information on the Family Law Courts website about how to appropriately undertake service. In essence, you need to organise for someone to hand a copy of the filed Application form to your spouse - you cannot be the person to hand it over.
6. Once the application is filed, a divorce hearing date will be issued.
7. You will only be required to attend the divorce hearing (which is usually by phone) if:

a. You asked to attend when completing the Application form.

b. The other party (the Respondent) asked to attend the hearing where:

i. there are children under the age of eighteen; or

ii. they have filed a Response to the Application, opposing it

c. You are applying for an Order for substituted service or a dispensation of service because you cannot find your spouse to serve the Court documents.

8. If there is a need for you to attend at the divorce hearing, it is a reasonably simple procedural event and occurs by phone. Normally someone at the Court will talk you through what you need to do. The hearing will be conducted by a Registrar. You should refer to the Registrar as 'Registrar' if you are asked to address them in any way. Listen to what they have to say and simply answer their questions. It is very common now for separating couples to act on their own behalf for a divorce hearing and the Court is quite used to this and will help you through the process. The Court appearance will generally only last about five minutes.

9. The divorce itself does not become effective until a month after the divorce hearing date. You will then be able to download a copy of the Divorce Certificate from the Court's online portal.

TIME LIMITATIONS AND OTHER CONSIDERATIONS

The important thing to remember is that, once you are divorced, you have only twelve months from that date to have either finalised your financial affairs, particularly your property settlement and any spousal maintenance arrangements, or to have at least commenced an application in one of the Family Courts if you and your partner can't reach an agreement.

The other important thing to remember with a divorce is that it can have a significant impact on any existing will, and you should get specific legal advice on that issue from a family or estate lawyer.

Many clients I have worked with never apply for their divorce – they don't plan on remarrying, so it is a step they just don't really bother with. Just keep in mind that it is important to formalise your financial settlement independent of your divorce, otherwise you might find your former partner coming along ten years after your separation seeking a share of your wealth!

PART THREE

The Legal Path All Roads Lead to a Document!

By choosing our path

we choose

our

destination.

UNKNOWN

The many ways to skin a cat

FINDING YOUR PATH TO AGREEMENT

No doubt you have at some stage heard a horror story about someone else's experience of divorce, whether it be the financial cost (sometimes hundreds of thousands of dollars) or the drawn-out legal process.

Where many separating couples get themselves into a bind very quickly is by not understanding that, no matter which path you take, you will likely end up with the same legal outcome. The central and most important difference is the 'path', or the road upon which you and your family travel to get to that legal outcome. If you choose a path such as the Court process, there is a high chance your experience of the legal process will be expensive, complicated and lengthy.

If, however, you choose a path such as mediation or collaborative practice, then while your journey may still be challenging, it will be less expensive and the outcome will be within your control.

There are essentially five different paths that you can choose to resolve your Family Law issues after your separation:

1. Reaching your own agreement or 'kitchen-table' negotiation
2. Negotiation through lawyers
3. Mediation
4. Collaborative practice
5. The Court process

Some families take one of these paths while others may choose to try a few different paths as they find their way. In this section, you'll learn about all five options, including the advantages and limitations of each.

IS THERE A PERFECT PATHWAY FOR YOUR FAMILY?

In my experience, it can take many years to travel through the emotional roller coaster of a divorce. The legal path that you and your spouse choose will have a significant impact on how quickly you can both move forward with your lives emotionally. If you end up in an antagonistic legal process, you will likely take a lot longer to move on with your life than those couples who have been able to negotiate and reach compromises early in their separation. However, there is no 'perfect' way to resolve your legal differences as what works really well for one family may be terrible for another.

In my experience it is combination of a few things that seem to work best in creating durable, inexpensive and appropriate legal agreements:

1. **A commitment to lasting relationships.** If you and your partner are genuinely committed to fostering your parenting relationship for your children, then this seems to flow into negotiations. Where the focus is on ensuring the best for the children, I see parents able to compromise, be flexible and see both sides of an outcome. While a lot of people say that they are genuinely committed to their children, in practice this is not always the case. If parents are more focused on their own agenda, settlements tend to take longer and quickly get muddied by irrelevant issues.
2. **Quality and expert advice.** When your team of advisers are all committed to resolution, there is a far greater chance your family will reach resolution. If your team of advisers includes lawyers who are focused on the Court path, then chances are that is the pathway your family will travel. Ensure that you are engaging advisers who are focused on pathways that meet your needs. For example, collaborative lawyers have undertaken specific training to ensure that they are able to effectively act for your family in this way. Similarly, mediators will have undertaken specific and extensive training in mediation and negotiation. Look at the skills of your advisers, ask for testimonials from their previous clients and don't be afraid to change advisers if you don't feel they are appropriate for you.

3. **Timing is everything.** An early settlement may be a great settlement, but sometimes the grief suffered after separation can make it too difficult for you or your partner to properly consider such significant legal matters. Do consider trying to reach an immediate holding pattern agreement for the three to six months after your separation to give you both time to obtain the information and advice you need to finalise your legal settlement. I have seen that where a holding pattern is reached quickly, final settlements tend to be achieved with far less angst. If there is no immediate agreement, I find clients are quickly drawn into big and expensive legal battles that are very hard to get out of down the track.

As you read the coming chapters, I encourage you to give a lot of thought to the type of path you wish your family to travel to settle your legal matters. If you have already engaged a family lawyer or are considering doing this, then take the time to discuss the pathways that they consider to be best for your circumstances.

Negotiation is a give and take process but being in control of the process is the only way to be successful at it.

CELSO CUKIERKORN

Pathway 1

REACHING YOUR OWN AGREEMENT A.K.A. KITCHEN-TABLE NEGOTIATIONS

By kitchen-table negotiations, I simply mean that you and your spouse agree on the terms of your separation agreement yourselves through discussion and direct negotiation. These discussions are often independent of any lawyers or other advisers; however, you may seek the advice and assistance of your advisers – either before starting these discussions or along the way.

This is a very cost-effective way of resolving your legal issues, but it is essential to seek legal advice after you have reached an agreement to ensure that your agreement is then drafted into an appropriate legally binding document. This is particularly the case in relation to financial matters, where there can be significant risks and costs if your legal matters are not properly finalised.

This form of direct negotiation is not for everyone but, more often than not, my clients have been able to discuss some of the legal issues with their spouse to reach a partial agreement – a common area where this occurs is in relation to home contents and personal items. Any agreements the two of you can reach yourselves will be beneficial at the end of the day. It is also often the case that once you start to agree on small things, discussing some of the bigger issues becomes easier.

How you and your partner are communicating will determine if this pathway is for you – if you cannot exchange an email without including a snipe or other negative comment, then avoid direct negotiations and engage a neutral party, such as a family lawyer or mediator, to assist you by facilitating your discussions and keeping you on track.

If you are going to try to negotiate directly with your spouse, consider meeting first with a specialist family lawyer to obtain an overview of the legal issues relating to your circumstances to ensure that you are not about to negotiate an agreement that is disadvantageous to you. I find it can be very challenging to 're-negotiate' an unfair agreement with a spouse who was to receive the benefit in the first place.

ELIZABETH'S STORY

It was my decision to end my marriage, and before I made that final decision I had met with a family lawyer to understand what to be aware of when I chose to leave so that I could be prepared.

This really helped me to then talk with my husband, Scott. He was really upset and in grief when I ended our marriage and was not really ready to talk to me about our property settlement.

I had received enough information and advice from meeting with my lawyer to know that I could give Scott time to come to grips with things. I stayed with friends and did my best to keep my communication with him civil. That was tough as he would call me or email me a lot and say some really hurtful things.

We discussed things mainly by email, and then one day we met up to talk about what we would do with our house and the money we had saved.

I think because I did not push things early on, it made it easier for Scott and me to agree when we were able to sit and talk together face-to-face.

I was able to do almost all the negotiation for myself and then took our agreement to my lawyers to be drafted and finalised.

If you are thinking about this type of negotiation, then consider these tips:

- **Prepare, Prepare, Prepare.** If you are meeting your former spouse to discuss significant issues, such as arrangements for your children or your property settlement, prepare as if it is a professional meeting. Take some notes, and prepare an agenda or checklist of the important things you would like to discuss. That way, if you get nervous or upset, you can turn to your list to get you back on track.

- **Compromise.** Be ready to compromise. If you are negotiating in person or by phone, it is sometimes best to take your spouse's proposal away to consider rather than responding on the spot (unless of course it is exactly what you had in mind!). Sometimes a few conversations or meetings will be necessary to give each of you time to consider the other's position and compromise where you can.
- **Start here but don't be afraid to try other pathways.** Sometimes this form of direct negotiation is a great place to start, but do try to get advice from a family lawyer before you begin and even along the way. If your conversation with your former spouse deteriorates or you cannot find your way through an issue, then it might be worth considering some of your other 'pathways' to agreement, such as mediation. The great thing about direct negotiation, such as kitchen-table negotiation, is that you can always come back to it and try again.

ADVANTAGES AND LIMITATIONS OF 'KITCHEN-TABLE' NEGOTIATIONS

ADVANTAGES	DISADVANTAGES
Minimal cost due to limited involvement from professional advisers.	Can lead to conflict if both parties are not able to communicate calmly.
You and your partner control the negotiation and therefore it can be done quite quickly.	Can be risky if you are not first aware of your legal rights and entitlements and perhaps are led into an agreement that is not entirely appropriate at law.
If you and your partner can agree on even small issues, it will really assist in developing a strong parenting relationship in the future.	If the agreement is not formalised, there may be legal and financial risks that arise in the future that you are not aware of right now.

We cannot solve our
problems
with the same
thinking
we used when
we created them.

ALBERT EINSTEIN

Pathway 2

LAWYER-ASSISTED NEGOTIATION

The second most common path that separating couples find themselves following is a lawyer-assisted negotiation, where family lawyers negotiate on behalf of their clients (the couple). This can be a very effective way of reaching an agreement, but can also come with its own array of pitfalls.

One of the central difficulties with lawyer-based negotiation is that you will rarely be in the driving seat of the negotiation. You are, in essence, handing your legal issues over to your adviser, who will then communicate on your behalf with either your partner or their adviser.

This style of negotiation will usually be done in writing, either by letter or email. It is the most common starting point if you are working with a family lawyer, but is also my least preferred 'pathway' as it can fast get out of hand both in time and cost. This pathway can be a good starting point to perhaps gather some information and make a settlement proposal, but it is often more cost and time effective to use the next two pathways - mediation or collaborative practice.

If you are using this pathway, there are a few things to consider:

- **Always be careful of the 'tone' of the communication that is sent.** I have received no end of legal correspondence in my time that is hurtful, harsh, inaccurate and unnecessary. If you are engaging a solicitor to negotiate on your behalf, remember that your partner will consider that professional to be an extension of you. Therefore, if that professional drafts and sends correspondence that is forceful or threatening, you can expect that this will set the tone of your negotiations from then on. Be very careful about the style, tone and content of correspondence that is sent on your behalf. Ask for your solicitor to forward letters being sent on your behalf to you and don't be afraid to seek amendments. You know your partner better than anyone. If you know that a comment in correspondence is likely to be considered hurtful by your partner, then ask for it to be removed or reworded. If you don't do this, there is a high chance that your partner will become distracted by that comment or the tone of the letter and will miss the central points you were trying to convey. There are no points to be won by sending correspondence that is threatening, and I can assure you that you will end up in a letter war that is unlikely to end in a peaceful resolution of your legal issues.
- **Be mindful of the timing of any legal correspondence.** In this day and age of instantaneous communication, an email can be sent and received in the space of a few seconds. I have seen the damage that can be done when a legal letter

is sent to an unsuspecting spouse who receives it at a most inopportune time. If you are having correspondence sent from your lawyer to your partner, discuss with your adviser how that might be sent and when it is likely to be received. Also consider speaking with your partner or perhaps emailing them in advance so that they are given the heads up to expect some legal documentation. Even the most politely drafted piece of legal correspondence can come as a significant shock to a newly separated and grief-stricken adult, so do be mindful of the bigger picture. Your correspondence should be designed to identify the legal issues and process that you would like to take, rather than being a place to apportion blame for past wrongdoings.

- **Remember the limitations of the written word.** A message drafted on paper, particularly in email, comes without the non-verbal cues through which we interpret the world. In my experience, so much more can be gained from a facilitated discussion or mediation than from the exchange of lengthy legal letters over several months. If you are engaging a family lawyer, consider setting a time frame in which you are willing to negotiate directly through your lawyer before you consider moving to an alternative path. Another option is to set a clear budget of what you are willing to spend on this form of negotiation. You might agree that you will engage your lawyer for four to six weeks to negotiate on your behalf before you both review whether this path is the best one for your circumstances. If it appears the letters are not being fruitful, then discuss with your lawyer whether facilitating a meeting with your partner and their adviser, or perhaps attending a mediation, may be a cheaper and quicker way of reaching a settlement.

While lawyer-assisted negotiation can help in the early stages of the legal process, it is often more cost effective and timely to consider mediation or collaboration as alternative ways of resolving your disputes, rather than exchanging letters for a lengthy period.

CAN WE HAVE A MEETING WITH OUR LAWYERS TOGETHER?

An alternative form of lawyer-assisted negotiation is what is often termed a 'round-table' or 'without-prejudice conference'. This is in essence a meeting on confidential terms between you, your spouse and your respective lawyers to discuss and try to resolve your legal issues. These sorts of meetings, when conducted properly, can be an effective way of resolving legal issues.

You don't necessarily need to sit in the same room or even at the same table, but the presence of both you and your spouse in the same building or virtual room can speed up discussions and negotiations and get to the heart of any disagreements very quickly. I would generally recommend that you consider a round-table negotiation in preference to the more traditional route of negotiating through correspondence and emails.

Sometimes a series of these meetings can be a fruitful way to reach an agreement on your legal issues. I recommend you speak with your lawyer and try to prepare an agenda before the meeting to ensure the main points you would like to discuss are covered. A few things to consider if you are preparing for or attending a without-prejudice conference are:

- **The time and location of the meeting.** If you know you or your partner need to collect your children each afternoon then be careful about the time you set for a meeting. To ensure that you can focus and won't be worrying about other issues, be clear about when you are available. The location of the meeting might also be important to you. Sometimes either lawyer's office is appropriate, or sometimes a neutral venue like a meeting centre might be more comfortable. Discuss these options with your adviser and make sure you know the physical location and set up for your meeting well before you attend. Also try to agree on the length of your meeting before you commence. In my experience, after two to three hours I find concentration wanes and meetings can quickly deteriorate into unproductive exchanges. If you set a clear timeframe and agenda at the outset, there is a far greater chance you will move through difficult issues and find agreements.
- **Preparation.** A face-to-face meeting with your former partner can sometimes be an incredibly daunting experience. To overcome this, take the time to prepare – confirm who will be attending, who is required to speak and what you might need to prepare before you attend. For example, if you are attending to discuss your financial settlement, should there be an exchange of financial documents before you attend or is this one of the things you might discuss during your meeting? Try to be clear about what you are going to discuss and what you hope to achieve before you attend. Remember – you can never over prepare!

In my day-to-day work as a family lawyer, lawyer-assisted negotiation is a mainstay of my business. Where you have two lawyers who know each other well and practise with a similar style, lasting agreements can be reached very quickly. However, this path to your settlement can become bumpy when the focus is not placed on resolution, or when a lawyer's communication style is unduly aggressive. It is important to consider the style of the lawyer you are engaging and ensure it fits with the type of legal negotiation and divorce approach you are hoping for.

ADVANTAGES AND LIMITATIONS OF SOLICITOR-ASSISTED NEGOTIATIONS

ADVANTAGES	DISADVANTAGES
Your legal rights and entitlements are protected as a trained professional will be negotiating on your behalf.	The style of the negotiation may be out of your hands - an unduly aggressive negotiation style can lead to further conflict rather than resolution.
Can be very cost effective where it involves solicitors who know and trust each other.	Timeframes can be difficult - you will be subject to the availability of your solicitor and, to some degree, your spouse's lawyer. This means it often will take two weeks to receive a response to correspondence. The turnaround time for negotiation by letter can be lengthy, which can quickly become very frustrating.
Removes you from the direct negotiation which can assist, particularly if there is conflict between you and your spouse or you are only in the early stages of your separation.	As there is little formality to this type of negotiation, it can last a long time and sometimes become very expensive very quickly - alternative options such as mediation should be considered if letters are not enabling you and your partner to find agreement.

In the middle of

difficulty

lies opportunity.

ALBERT EINSTEIN

Pathway 3

MEDIATION

Mediation has fast become the most common path that separating couples now use to resolve their legal issues. There are many different types and styles of mediation available now; however, generally the term describes a process where you and your spouse meet with an independent person (the mediator) who will facilitate discussions between you and assist you both to reach agreement.

There are many different forms of mediation available to families after separation. A few of the most common types of mediation that you might encounter include family dispute resolution, private mediation and child-inclusive mediation.

FAMILY DISPUTE RESOLUTION

'Family dispute resolution' is a phrase often used to describe mediation where parents are attending to discuss their parenting arrangements. It is now compulsory to participate in a form of family dispute resolution in Australia before you commence proceedings in a Family Court (unless there is risk to you or your children, or urgency).

Family dispute resolution is offered by a range of community organisations, such as Relationships Australia, and government-funded centres called 'Family Relationship Centres'. Most cities and large towns will have a Family Relationship Centre where this form of mediation is offered either at no cost or a very low cost. Along with mediation, these centres also offer courses, counselling and other ancillary services to assist you after your separation.

There are also a number of mediators working in their own businesses who offer family dispute resolution. A quick Google search in your local area for a 'family dispute resolution provider' should help you find a local professional, and you can check their qualifications on the Attorney General's website: www.fdrr.ag.gov.au/fdrr.

PRIVATE MEDIATION

'Private mediation' is a term used in the legal industry to refer to a mediation process provided by a paid mediator who works outside the centres referred to previously. As mediation is now the most common way separating couples deal with their legal matters, there are an ever-increasing number of mediators entering the market to service this growing need. As such, there are a wide variety of mediators available to assist you, but they do tend to bring with them a differing array of skills. The cost of your mediator will also vary depending on their professional background and skill.

Mediators come primarily from two backgrounds - the social scientists (counsellors, social workers and psychologists) and lawyers (family lawyers, barristers and often retired Judges). The type of mediator you need will depend on the issues you have to resolve. For example, if you and your spouse are in the early stages of your separation, have largely agreed on most issues and are seeking assistance in formalising arrangements for your children, a social scientist may be appropriate to ensure that the needs of your children are considered. However, if you have been involved in legal negotiations for some time that seem to have stalled, engaging a lawyer with expertise in the Family Law, who is also a mediator, is often the best option to assist you both to reach a resolution.

There is no 'right or wrong' option when it comes to your mediator. Some social scientists have been working in the Family Law area for many years and have strong legal knowledge to complement their specialities. Similarly, many lawyer mediators are well able, through their training and experience, to balance an understanding of the complexities of the law with the understanding needed to assist families and children at this difficult time.

CHILD-INCLUSIVE MEDIATION

This form of mediation may sound like it means your children are coming to the mediation with you, but that is not quite the case. In a child-inclusive mediation there will be two separate professionals involved – your mediator and a child expert (normally a social worker or psychologist with expertise in Family Law matters). In this case, you, your partner and your children will first meet with a child expert who will take some time to talk with you all to understand the issues that need resolution for your family. That professional will then attend your mediation to provide you and your partner with feedback about how your children are coping with your separation and what arrangements might work best for them in the future. This professional is not your mediator. They will, however, work with your mediator to assist you and your partner to find a resolution.

This form of mediation is still new to many family lawyers, but is something I would highly recommend to parents who are struggling to find agreements on their parenting arrangements. Having independent input on what might work best for your children and hearing how they feel about your separation is a powerful way of breaking an impasse between you and your partner. Generally, your children will not tell either of you exactly what they are really thinking, as they often don't want to hurt you or be involved in your dispute. However, children often open up to a trained professional. I have also seen the feedback some parents receive in these mediations to be incredibly reassuring! In a recent example, I observed my client, a father, walk away from a child-inclusive mediation with confidence that, despite the complete breakdown in communication between him and his former wife, his two girls were coping well. In this family the girls had reported to their father that they were at risk, and he was quite rightly very concerned about their welfare. We learned during the mediation process that in fact the girls were not at risk. They just wanted their parents back together and had started to say things to their parents that were not necessarily true, but were designed to get their attention and hopefully, in the children's minds, result in the separation ending and their family being whole again.

For this family, the mediation process itself enabled them to re-establish a dialogue between the parents so that they could support their girls but also work together to help the children understand that, while their marriage had ended, they were still a family. The involvement of a psychologist as an independent child expert was instrumental in creating an environment where the parents trusted the information that was provided.

I would strongly recommend this process if you and your spouse cannot agree on issues relating to the time your children might spend with each of you or have different views about how your children should be raised. Keep in mind, of course, that you may receive feedback that you don't expect, but if you are focused on getting to the bottom of your issues and actually solving the points of difference, then this is a really worthwhile way to do it.

JASON'S STORY

The breakdown of my marriage has been both the most trying and uncertain time of my adult life. After being with my wife for thirteen years I made the hard decision to value my own happiness and move forward in a positive direction.

However, I knew that there would be repercussions impacting my daughters, aged five and eight. I would no longer be with them on a full-time basis to manage their day-to-day lives. After our separation I was struggling with a lack of cooperation from my ex-wife. We had barely any civil communication. I was experiencing extreme levels of frustration and anxiety about the health and safety of my children while they were not in my care.

My lawyer suggested that we try child-inclusive mediation and to my surprise it was a very rewarding experience. The great thing for me was that instead of drawn-out negotiations that often got nasty with no positive result, this process was completed over two days, one with the clinical psychologist and one mediation day with all parties involved. It gave me reassurance that my children were talking to an expert in child psychology who had 'seen and heard it all before' and who had their best interests at heart. It is true I did not hear everything that I wanted to hear and made some compromises during this process, but the relief that I felt walking out at the end of the day was enormous. I have confidence that the agreement we reached that day will ensure that my daughters' wellbeing is the main priority moving forward.

TIPS WHEN CHOOSING YOUR MEDIATOR

When it comes to choosing your mediator, keep the following in mind:

1. **Consider your budget.** Most mediators charge on an hourly basis, and some require a minimum booking of several hours. Services such as Family Relationship Centres and organisations like Relationships Australia can be a very cost-effective and accessible option, particularly where budget is a concern. It is also helpful to think about the complexity of your situation and the kind of support you may need. In some cases, engaging a specialist family lawyer as a mediator can be beneficial, particularly where there are more complex legal, financial or parenting issues to work through. While a mediator cannot provide legal advice to either party, an experienced family lawyer-mediator can help identify legal issues as they arise and encourage you to obtain

independent advice where appropriate. Ultimately, the aim is to choose a mediator whose skills, experience and approach are well suited to your circumstances. Doing so can help support a durable and workable agreement, and may reduce the likelihood of needing to revisit issues later.

2. **Consider your timing.** The timing of any negotiation is essential to its success. A series of mediations can be more effective than one big day of intense negotiation, and often this will not be any more expensive. In my experience an 'early' mediation to assist you and your partner to reach an interim agreement or that 'holding pattern' I wrote about in Part 1 is the best way to stay on the path to resolution. If you can agree on immediate living arrangements, parenting arrangements and financial matters, you can both then take some time to gather any more information you might need, get legal and financial advice and then meet for another mediation to discuss and, hopefully, resolve your legal issues.

   Keep in mind that if one of you is not emotionally ready to negotiate, a mediation will become very difficult very quickly. If you are not ready to sit and have a discussion about finalising your legal matters, then do consider seeking professional assistance from a counsellor to help you through. The sooner you can start to participate in discussions about matters that are important to you, the sooner you will start to feel back in control of your life, which is essential to be able to move forward from your separation. Similarly, if it is your spouse who is not ready or is even unwilling to attend mediation with you, then don't give up. Try to give them some space to process their emotions. As long as you both have somewhere to live, financial support and time with your children, you should be able to wait a few weeks. If not, then seek assistance from a mediator or family lawyer to discuss the most effective way to engage with your partner during the initial difficult period.

3. **Consider the issues that need to be resolved.** If your dispute relates to financial matters that include complex business or investment structures, then I would strongly recommend obtaining legal advice and engaging a mediator with a legal background. The legal ramifications of dividing businesses, companies, trusts and property can be very expensive if not done properly. If, however, you and your partner want to discuss matters relating to your children, it may be that a social scientist, such as a psychologist, would be the right sort of mediator for you.

4. **Research, research, research.** Thanks to our modern world it is now easy to Google a wealth of information about a mediator you may wish to engage. A personal referral from a trusted professional is a good place to start but, failing this, jump online and start looking. Think about what style of mediator might be right for your family. Most will have websites that include articles and information about their background and services. Don't be afraid to call them and have a general chat about their process and what you can expect. This is often the best way to tell immediately if you can generate a rapport with someone. If your partner has already chosen a mediator, don't be afraid to call them and get an understanding of what you can expect if you engage their services.

THE ROLLS ROYCE OF MEDIATION SERVICES

If money was not an issue, I would recommend that anyone trying to finalise the legal matters arising from their separation and divorce consider what I call the 'Rolls Royce mediation model'. I call it that as, unsurprisingly, this will often be the most expensive mediation option. However, just like a Rolls Royce, there are significant benefits that come from the financial investment. If you have engaged a family lawyer and they have spoken to you about mediation, then there is every chance it is this type of mediation they have described (although they probably have not called it the Rolls Royce model!). Similarly, if you have already found yourself in the Family Courts, this is the type of mediation that a Judge will often order you to attend in the early stages of the Court process. In this model you will have:

- You and your family lawyer
- Your former partner and their family lawyer
- A mediator (who is usually another family lawyer)
- Other professionals as needed (such as child psychologists, financial planners, accountants)

This form of mediation is most commonly used by the legal profession when we are assisting families to resolve legal issues, largely because of the high settlement rates that arise from this style of mediation. The involvement of a team of professionals, including a highly qualified mediator, will give you and your family the best environment to discuss and resolve legal issues.

This style of mediation works best when:

- You and your partner have engaged legal representatives;
- You have not been able to agree on significant issues (such as the division of your finances or the time your children might spend with each of you); and
- When you have had time to prepare all the information you will need to make a decision, compromise and reach agreement (for example, you have exchanged financial information, and have obtained valuations of your assets, such as your home and the like).

A significant advantage of the 'Rolls Royce' mediation process is that it can be customised to suit your family's needs.

Do take the time to speak with your family lawyer about the style of mediation that is best suited to you. Don't be afraid to ask why they are recommending a particular type of mediation over another. Be involved in the decision-making process, understand how your mediation process will work and, most importantly, ensure you are involved in the preparation for the day. You should attend your mediation knowing and understanding what your best and worst legal outcomes might be. You should also have discussed your negotiation strategy with your lawyer prior to attending and be ready to make and consider any settlement proposals. Most importantly, keep an open mind, remain positive and be ready to compromise.

ADVANTAGES AND DISADVANTAGES OF MEDIATION	
ADVANTAGES	**DISADVANTAGES**
You and your partner have more control over the legal outcome when compared to the Court process where a Judge will decide your legal outcome.	There are very few limitations of the mediation process. I have struggled to see almost any disadvantage as such, so instead will focus on what I have seen can be the barriers to settlement that you may encounter if you choose to proceed with mediation: • Perhaps the most significant is the impact of unrealistic expectations on your mediation outcome. If you or your partner attends a mediation event without a complete understanding of the risks of failing to reach a settlement, this can have a negative impact on the settlement discussions. If one of you has had legal advice and the other has not, this may mean that one of you is not yet abreast of the limitations of your legal position and is making offers that are just not realistic. If your legal issues relate to financial matters, you should both obtain independent legal advice before attending mediation to ensure that you have a full understanding of the likely range of legal outcomes in your situation. • The second barrier to settlement I have experienced is poor preparation. Again, this is more often than not in financial matters where offers are exchanged for one party to refinance the family home, but that person has not been to a bank to establish whether they have the financial capacity to undertake the proposal. Try to ensure you are over-prepared before you attend a mediation. Make enquiries with your financiers to ensure that you know where your limitations are or the impact on you and your partner of selling or transferring assets.

ADVANTAGES AND DISADVANTAGES OF MEDIATION	
The financial cost of the mediation process is significantly less than the Court process. Even a Rolls Royce mediation will cost far less than one or two trials in the Court process.	
Mediation can be conducted very quickly - this is perhaps the most significant advantage - more often than not mediation is conducted in one day and if an agreement is reached your legal issues are then resolved. It is a very quick process and you and your partner have control over the timing of your mediation event.	The skills of your chosen mediator are essential to the success of your mediation. Take the time to ensure that you have chosen an experienced mediator. Seek testimonials and input from your advisers. If your lawyer is nominating a mediator, ask why they consider them to be the right fit for your case. A talented mediator will balance legal knowledge with personal skill. The skill is in making you and your partner feel comfortable and empowered to make difficult decisions in what can be a pressured environment. A mediator is not there to give you legal advice or push you into a settlement. They may, however, reality-test proposals or identify some pitfalls.
It is a simple and flexible process and should feel comfortable and fluid. A skilled mediator will enable you to feel relaxed and in control of your outcome. There are no complicated rules or procedures like those in the Court process.	

Tell me
and I forget.
Teach me
and I remember.
Involve me
and I learn.

BENJAMIN FRANKLIN

Pathway 4

COLLABORATIVE PRACTICE

Collaborative Practice is the name given to a process of dispute resolution that is, in essence, a series of meetings between you, your spouse and your respective lawyers to discuss the issues between you and reach agreement. Essential to the collaborative process is the commitment by you, your spouse and your lawyers to focus on settlement outcomes and not threaten or commence Court proceedings. The commitment to settlement is what separates the collaborative process from mediation or a round-table conference conducted as part of lawyer-assisted negotiations.

This commitment is documented in the form of a binding contract - this means that all the participants in your collaborative process (you, your partner, your legal advisers and other professional advisers) are committing to focus purely on settlement options, and through the contract agree not to go to Court or even threaten Court proceedings. In the event that the settlement process breaks down and the collaborative team disbands, then you and your partner will have the opportunity to engage new legal advisers to enter the Court process.

Family lawyers who are collaborative lawyers have undertaken significant training to enable them to work in this model. It does require a shift for lawyers, who will use skills that are perhaps not utilised as much in lawyer-assisted negotiation or in litigation.

The collaborative process works well for families who are focused on maintaining relationships, particularly as parents, in the future. It offers significant advantages for couples to create a bespoke process and agreement after separation. I would best describe it as the pathway for those seeking a 'dignified' and 'respectful' divorce process.

The collaborative process is also very useful in both parenting and financial matters, as it allows for significant flexibility and can offer families the benefit of advice from professionals such as financial planners and accountants, as well as counsellors and child experts, to ensure that their legal matters are settled in the most beneficial way for the whole family.

In collaborative practice, the negotiations generally occur through a series of two-hour meetings. In my experience, it takes two to five meetings for a couple to reach agreement on a final basis in relation to financial and parenting issues.

Perhaps the most significant difference between collaborative practice and the other pathways I have mentioned is the focus on your goals and interests in the collaborative process. Unlike the remaining legal pathways, in a collaborative process you and your spouse will be able to focus on your goals and values, and will be encouraged to discuss agreements that meet those interests but also meet your legal entitlements and obligations. As a result of this, I find that the agreements reached in the collaborative process are often more holistic and long-lasting, as they are personalised to the couple and their family.

ROBERT'S STORY

After separating from my wife and deciding that we ultimately saw no future in our marriage, we both knew we would need to work together in the future for the benefit of our two boys.

We decided on a collaborative approach to the divorce process, which included the property settlement. Although there had been pain in the break up, we put this aside and worked out amicably how we would share our property, the custody of our children and the finances for doing so.

My wife had her lawyer, I had mine and over a number of joint meetings held around a table we worked out the best solution for everyone, including bringing in experts as required to value any items that we both thought should have an independent valuation. My accountant was also involved, which really helped to ensure we had the information we needed about my business to make decisions together.

While there were some tense moments, the outcome meant we could move on with our respective lives far sooner than if we had gone down the more traditional Court route. We just really wanted to avoid the drama and the added cost of lawyers going backwards and forwards.

It took us around four months to finalise things and, some five years on from our divorce, I talk to my ex-wife about my boys on a weekly basis, we share time together with them at their birthdays, weekend sports and the occasional meal.

I think the collaborative process worked really well for my family. It enabled my former wife and I to be in charge of our negotiations and to tailor a solution for our family that fit with the lives we both had planned for our boys.

ADVANTAGES AND LIMITATIONS OF COLLABORATIVE PRACTICE

ADVANTAGES	DISADVANTAGES
You are committed to staying away from the Court process, therefore saving both financial and emotional cost.	Collaborative practice is not for everyone. If either you or your partner is not genuinely committed to the process, it simply will not work. If either of you are: • Looking for an easy option, • Hiding information, or • Seeking revenge, then this pathway is not for your family. Collaborative practice will have limited success in these situations.

ADVANTAGES AND LIMITATIONS OF COLLABORATIVE PRACTICE

Collaborative practice enables a bespoke settlement process and outcome for families. By working within a team you will benefit from the legal and professional expertise of all the parties at the table – meaning that both your lawyer and your spouse's lawyer are working together to solve your legal differences. This often means that many more solutions are generated and more creative and individual settlement outcomes are created.	Perhaps the most significant limitation associated with collaborative practice is the idea that if your settlement discussions break down, then you and your partner will need to stop this process and will have to engage new lawyers to start the Court process. The significant disadvantage in this is the perceived additional cost in doing this. In my experience, very few collaborative matters do not reach resolution. However, if it does not work for you, the time and money invested in the settlement discussions is rarely wasted, as during your collaborative process you will have narrowed your legal issues and at least got a better understanding of where your points of difference are. As such, if you find yourself having to move into either mediation or the Court process, you will find that you will be able to move through those processes a lot quicker.
At the heart of the collaborative process is the balancing of the goals, interests and values of you and your partner with your legal rights and entitlements. Therefore what is actually important to your family (where you want to live, your future plans, perhaps your retirement plan) will form the agenda for your legal discussions. Any legal settlement will be structured around your goals and values. It is this personal focus in collaborative practice that creates lasting and valuable settlement outcomes.	
The involvement of professionals such as counsellors, child experts, financial planners, accountants and the like sets collaborative practice aside from all other legal processes. Being able to obtain professional input from a team of likeminded advisers will enable your family to create tailored and lasting solutions while ensuring a holistic approach is taken, thereby considering all the matters arising from your separation, not just your legal differences.	

Law is reason free from passion.

ARISTOTLE

Pathway 5

LITIGATION – THE COURT PROCESS

A colleague and dear friend of mine aptly describes the Court process as 'The Land of the Law' – a magical mystery land that has its own rules, regulations and rulers who even wear fancy dress. Unless you are a legal practitioner, chances are your understanding of the Court process comes from courtroom dramas that fill primetime television slots. The reality is that it is a daunting, strange place full of etiquette, tradition and a language that is very hard to understand unless you work there, day in and day out.

Most of us have heard some sort of horror story about encounters with the Family Law Courts. If you are entering the Court system, I see only one advantage – you are buying a decision maker. You are paying a very large amount of money so that a stranger can make a decision about the things that are most important to you. However, while those strangers are intelligent, caring and wise people, they don't have magic wands and are certainly not magicians. A Judge will carefully and appropriately apply their legal knowledge to the facts of your case, apply legal principle and make a decision about the matters you ask of them. While this might sound simple, it is not.

WHAT TO EXPECT

There are essentially three primary Courts in Australia that administer the Family Law Act:

- The Federal Circuit and Family Court of Australia Division 1 and 2 (the 'Family Law Courts')
- The Local or Magistrates Court

Most matters are now dealt with in the Federal Circuit and Family Court of Australia Division 2. More complex matters will be dealt with by the Federal Circuit and Family Court of Australia Division 1. For ease, I refer to these two Courts, which operate out of the same buildings, as the 'Family Courts'. If you are going to Court, it won't matter too much to you if you are in Division 1 or Division 2, as they really are very similar. If you live in a remote area your local Court may initially deal with your Family Law matter, particularly if there is not a Family Court close by.

The Family Courts are generally located in major cities around Australia, but much of the process is now delivered online. I work from Brisbane but can assist clients all over Australia, as many of the Court appearances can be undertaken via phone or video. (One of the few upsides of the strange events that came with Covid.)

Generally, simply getting into Court can take some time.

Before you can start you must comply with what are called 'Pre-Action Procedures'. These include making a genuine effort to try to resolve your legal issues and attending mediation.

If you have completed those requirements and been unable to settle your case, you can then commence an Application, which involves preparing a series of documents that are filed with the Court. It can take several weeks, and sometimes months to prepare those documents. If you are working with a family lawyer, make sure you get them the information they need to make the process as streamlined as possible.

Once you have filed your documents it will usually take another eight to twelve weeks before you have your first day in Court.

That first Court date is before a Registrar and often somewhat procedural. I think of the first Court date as much like a triage moment in an emergency room at a hospital. The Registrar is trying to get a general understanding of the legal issues that need to be resolved and move your case to the best next step. As such, often not much happens on this first Court date, but a plan will be put in place for what happens from there.

For example, if your application is in relation to property and financial issues, it is common for Orders to be made for the exchange of information or the valuation of certain property items. If your application is about parenting matters, there will likely be an Order for you, your spouse and children to see a social worker or psychologist for interviews for a child impact report or a family report that will assist the Judge in better understanding your family and your children.

The Court process includes a series of these short hearings, called 'mentions', as the Court tries to ensure that they have the information required to enable them to make a decision at a trial. This also ensures that you and your partner have the information needed to come to an arrangement yourself. It is also common for the Court to require you to attend mediation during your Court process, even if you participated in mediation before.

As you move through the Court process, Orders will be made at each Court event. Whatever those Orders say, comply with them. If you are found to have not complied with a Court Order you can end up in a legal pickle very quickly and there can be significant consequences.

If you and your partner are unable to reach an agreement after all the relevant information has been gathered, your case will go to trial. The trial is the big event, the opportunity where you and your spouse present your legal arguments to the Judge. You will then be cross examined by barristers and, ultimately, the Judge will make a determination about the matters you have raised.

The Court will then issue Orders setting out how your finances might be divided or how much time your children will spend between each of you.

HOW TO BEHAVE

Be respectful throughout the process, even if things are not going your way. Your conduct is on display at all times in the Court building or online, so be mindful of your actions and reactions. If you are with a lawyer they will do the majority of the talking to the Court on your behalf; however, if you are representing yourself or are asked a direct question, refer to the Judge as 'Your Honour' or the Registrar as 'Registrar'. If you are in the Court building, stand when you are talking. If you are online, make sure you have privacy, and you can easily be seen and heard.

Your role in this process is to present the relevant factual information that your Judge needs to know to determine your case in your favour. This information is given in writing, by way of an 'affidavit'. Only 'relevant' facts will be of any importance to a Judge deciding your matter. As we have a no-fault legal system, the fact that your partner may have caused you significant hurt through adultery during your marriage is rarely a fact that is relevant to the Court's determination of your case.

To support these facts you will need to supply 'admissible evidence'. There are many rules about what constitutes admissible evidence that are confusing to even the brightest legal minds. As a result, even if you know something to be the truth, unless you can establish it in Court by way of admissible evidence and provable relevant facts, a Judge may not agree with you.

Keeping this focus on relevant factual information and admissible evidence in mind, you don't want to become emotional if possible. Focus on sharing facts and evidence, and ensure you are prepared to do this - have your documents filed, ordered and easy to find, and have them with you at all times. Make sure you have a pen and paper so that you can take notes and write down important dates. If you can sit in the back of the Court or listen to some other cases online before you have to appear, you can get an understanding of the approach of the Judge or Registrar in your case, know where to sit and hear what other people are saying. This will mean you can focus on your case when it's your turn.

Finally, keep in mind that Courts are formal places, so dress professionally. Long sleeves or jackets and long pants are appropriate for men, while longer skirts, pants and dresses with jackets are also appropriate for women.

SO HOW LONG WILL IT TAKE?

How long is a piece of string? I can tell you one thing - the legal process moves slowly. It will generally take at least eighteen months to reach a trial. Once you have had your trial, which might last over a few days, you are unlikely to receive the Judge's decision for some months. They will generally 'reserve their decision' or, in other words, go away and think about things before making a final determination. In some instances it can take a further two years after a trial to receive your decision, which means the entire process may be up to four years.

Just pause for a moment and imagine how you feel right now – the uncertainty, the fear, the grief... Imagine staying in that state for another four years as you wind your way down the yellow brick road that is the magical mystery land of the law. Imagine not moving on for the next four years – not changing your finances in any significant way, not knowing where you'll be living in the long term, not having access to joint assets... Just imagine how that might feel. I expect it would be terrible.

HOW MUCH WILL IT COST?

It is almost easy to quantify the financial cost of the Court process in terms of the amount you might spend on legal fees. From beginning to end expect it to be at least $150,000, each. When I wrote the first edition of this book I estimated legal fees to be $50,000 each. In that ten years I have seen the costs of the legal process increase exponentially. Whatever the cost, it is a huge amount of money and something you should keep in mind when choosing this option.

It is much harder to quantify the indirect financial costs and the significant emotional costs involved in pursuing your personal family matters in the Court system. Think about the cycle of grief discussed in Part 1 – if you are fighting your former partner in the Court process for up to four years, there is a very strong chance you will both remain in the grief cycle moving between anger and depression. These feelings will not be isolated to your legal issues – they will flow into all aspects of your daily life, including your work and personal life and, most importantly, they will affect your children.

You will also be required to take time off work for meetings and Court attendances. Your children may also be required to speak with professionals about their experience of your divorce. Your capacity as a parent, no matter how good you are, will come into the spotlight, which is confronting and upsetting. All of this will take a significant emotional toll that is very hard to quantify.

WHAT DO YOU HAVE TO DO BEFORE YOU CAN GET THERE?

For a whole range of reasons it is now more difficult than ever to just 'take someone to Court'. This is primarily because it is accepted by the Courts themselves that most families should not need the assistance of Judges to resolve their Family Law matters. It is now compulsory that you and your spouse have participated in mediation in relation to parenting issues before you commence proceedings in a Family Court. While it is not yet compulsory to undertake mediation for financial matters, it is necessary that you have at least made some reasonable attempt to reach a resolution. Further, most Courts will make Orders on the first Court date for you and your spouse to attend mediation to discuss your financial matters, if you have not already done so prior to coming to Court.

REMEMBER TO SEEK ADVICE

If you do find yourself in the Family Court process, then ensure you obtain specialist advice from a family lawyer. Courts are complicated places and it is not something that I would recommend tackling without the assistance of a lawyer. If you simply cannot afford the services of a family lawyer, then contact your local Legal Aid office to see if they can assist you. If Legal Aid is not an option, then there are many community legal centres that will assist you at no cost – they may not attend Court with you, but they can advise you on the preparation of documents and what to expect when you go to Court.

WHATEVER YOU DO, AVOID THE COURT PROCESS

KYLIE'S STORY

'Going to Court was emotionally exhausting. It wasn't just that it became about 'winning', instead of about our children, or that the ultimate decision was taken out of my hands. It was because I had to read all the hateful things my ex thinks about me, including his lies. I had to find a way to not let him see that I was upset by what he wrote.

I also had to keep everything that was happening from my children. When I was feeling anxious or angry or sad, my kids knew something was wrong, but I couldn't talk to them about it honestly. It was hard to reassure them about what was happening when I wasn't sure what was going to happen. I was scared and anxious and worried and alone. The only other person who could really relate to what I was going through was my ex-husband – but he was my 'enemy', not my friend.

The time between filing my Court material and the trial day was like living in purgatory. It was an interim place where I couldn't make plans for after the trial date, because I didn't know when our children would be with me. In itself, this was torturous – I was waiting to find out if my legal team could convince a Judge that my argument was more persuasive than my ex-husband's argument. There was no right or wrong, just an expert's opinion of what was best for my children. The Judge didn't meet my children and the Court expert only interviewed them for about ten minutes each. The rest of our life as a family felt as though it relied solely on what the family report writer learned from one interview. That isn't to say that what the report writer found wasn't accurate, but it was just a tiny snapshot of who my children are and how they felt – a year before the trial! It wasn't just the Court expert and Judge who held our fate. It was also my lawyers. I had to implicitly trust that what I was being told was right and going to work.

I had no control over what was happening, what decision was made or how to approach any of it. I was totally at the mercy of the very expensive professionals I was paying. If divorce is like death, Court is like hell.'

Kylie's story is not isolated. Almost every client I have seen experience the Family Court process feels just as she did.

While the Court process can, for some families, be an appropriate path for resolution of Family Law issues, it should be considered as your last resort, or only used in emergencies.

The financial and emotional costs of the Court process are great. It is very unlikely that you and your spouse will have any chance of a friendship or good parenting relationship after a three-day trial where your legal advisers have just done everything they can to destroy each of you and paint you in the worst possible light.

However, the greatest risk of any Court application is the lack of control you have over the outcome. There are an awful lot of ducks that need to form a row to 'win' in the Family Court process, and once you step into a courtroom you are handing over your right to make decisions about your financial affairs and your children. These are generally the two most important things in our lives.

Fortunately, you and your partner can control how you engage with the legal system and, as I've discussed in this section, there are other options. While the Family Law Courts administer the Family Law in our country, the vast majority (around ninety per cent) of separating families never require the assistance of the Courts to determine their Family Law issues.

If you do end up in Court, try to use the Court process as a way of reaching an agreement with your former partner. Often Court proceedings are commenced because one party to a failed relationship is simply refusing to participate in negotiations. They might be withholding information or simply burying their head in the sand hoping things will 'just go away'. Often your first Court date is a good opportunity to set in place some tools that will help you and your partner to bridge any impasses, such as Orders for the exchange of documents, or a family report to help you understand the best parenting arrangements for your children. Because these Orders are made throughout the hearings (or 'mentions'), around ninety-five per cent of the cases that start in the Family Courts reach settlement somewhere along the way. This means that even if you are already in the Court process, there is still a very high chance you can reach an agreement without having to experience a trial.

ADVANTAGES AND LIMITATIONS OF THE COURT PROCESS

ADVANTAGES	DISADVANTAGES
Will ensure a decision is made on your legal issues.	Can take a significant amount of time - generally between eighteen months and four years to reach a final conclusion.
Can provide a 'structure', particularly where one spouse is not participating in negotiations or is being dishonest.	Can cost very large amounts of money to meet the legal fees of having lawyers represent you (upwards of $50,000).
Can provide safety in circumstances where children or adults are at risk of harm and can also be appropriate in circumstances where something has occurred that required urgent legal intervention - for example the removal of children or the sale of significant assets.	Will generally mean that you and your former partner will remain in conflict for the duration of your Court proceeding, which will affect your capacity to work together at the end of your Court matter. This in turn will affect your children, who will no doubt be exposed to or be aware of the conflict.
	The Court process can be very confusing and is often not 'lineal'. In other words, there will be speed bumps that mean you will feel like things are moving slowly and are often out of your control.

When does
the art of compromise
become
compromising?

SARAH JESSICA PARKER

Communicate, negotiate and compromise

No matter which legal process you and your spouse choose, at some stage you will need to negotiate an outcome in relation to your legal issues. Negotiation is an art that could fill a book all on its own, but there are a few key tips that you should keep in mind when you're preparing for your negotiation.

If you have engaged a family lawyer, then chances are they will undertake the majority of the negotiations on your behalf. However, a good family lawyer will continually consult with you and seek your guidance as to how you wish to move forward in your negotiations. They should also discuss negotiation styles with you to formulate a negotiation strategy that works for your family.

Before becoming a family lawyer, I had a perception, thanks to primetime TV shows, that divorce settlements were negotiated across a big boardroom table, with two lawyers and two clients bartering over possessions and belongings.

During my career I have never seen this occur. Most negotiations, particularly if they are guided by family lawyers, will occur through correspondence or through the exchange of proposals and offers in a verbal sense at a formal negotiation such as mediation.

However, when guided by family lawyers, the process of negotiation can become confusing and expensive very quickly. If you have engaged a lawyer, do speak to them openly about the strategy that they recommend, what steps you can take to assist and how to minimise your costs.

NEGOTIATION STYLES

What to avoid - I want it all! Positional bargaining

Negotiating your property settlement or the arrangements for your children should not become like bartering at a market for cheap goods. I have had clients, particularly in property settlement matters, who said to me, 'Look I'd be happy to receive something like $100,000, so the offer we should put in is $150,000 and it should probably settle at $100,000.' Sometimes that's true, but if at the end of the day the total asset pool that the two of you are negotiating is only $160,000 and you start with an opening offer of $150,000, you can expect that your former partner will be somewhat frustrated, angry and perhaps even offended by your offer.

You can also expect that, in response, your former partner will pick an extreme position – in other words, he or she will pick a number that is far outside the range of what they expect to receive with a view to meeting a compromise somewhere in the middle. This will cause you frustration and anger and, before you know it, the two of you are pitted against each other, either exchanging emails, letters or expensive legal correspondence as you try to bridge the gap.

As much as possible, you want to avoid this form of negotiation, or 'positional bargaining'. As children we become particularly talented at positional bargaining – I take a position, I establish rules and I don't move until I achieve what I want. I'll bargain with you so that I ensure that I retain my position. It's something we're taught from an early age and it's hard to lose, particularly in difficult situations. It is, however, a very simplistic form of negotiation and something you want to avoid at all costs.

The better way – interest-based negotiation

A better way of negotiating is interest-based negotiation. While it sounds fancy, it just means trying to understand what your spouse really wants – their underlying goals or needs – and using those as a guide to try to formulate proposals that will meet them.

Earlier in this book, you undertook some exercises that helped you to work out your goals as well as your spouse's goals. You will need this information to negotiate using interest-based negotiation. The great thing about interest-based negotiation is that, once you understand how to do it, you will use it in every aspect of your life – at work, at home and particularly with teenagers!

I often use this simple story to illustrate how interest-based negotiation works in practice, which was made famous by the authors Roger Fisher and William Ury in their book *Getting to Yes: Negotiating an Agreement Without Giving In.*[1] It's a great book and worth reading not only for your divorce negotiations, but for any negotiation you need to undertake in any setting:

> Imagine there are two young children fighting over an orange and their mother comes in. Mum asks, 'What's the problem? What do you want?' and the kids both say, 'I want the orange!'
>
> Mum takes the orange, chops it in half and then gives half to each child and says, 'There you go, stop fighting.' The two children turn around and they're still upset and sad. The mother asks the kids, 'What's wrong?'
>
> Little Mary says, 'Mum, I needed a whole cup of orange juice because I have to make a cake for school tomorrow and without the whole orange, I can't make my cake.'
>
> Then little Bob says to Mum, 'Mum, I needed a whole orange full of seeds and without all of the seeds from the orange I won't be able to finish my science experiment this week and now I've only got half.'
>
> The moral to the story – had Mum just asked why the children needed the orange, both of their needs could have been met. Mary could have had a cupful of orange juice while Bob could have had an orange full of seeds, both from the same orange, both meeting their needs without the need for fighting. It was just important to understand why each child needed the orange.

---

1 Fisher, R & Ury, W 1991, Getting to Yes: Negotiating Agreement without Giving In, 2nd edn, Penguin Group, New York, New York.

Now I appreciate that this is a simplistic analogy, but I use it almost every day in my work. When I act for clients who are in dispute over property settlement matters, I spend a lot of time trying to understand why my client is seeking the outcome they're after. No one is ever seeking sixty per cent – what they're actually seeking is financial security, somewhere to live, control of their life and to minimise change. If a client or their spouse is saying, 'I must keep the home,' it's very rare that they genuinely want only that home. More often than not, what they're really after is a home that provides them with security in a particular area where all of their friends and social networks are.

The same can be said for negotiating arrangements for children. If a parent is saying that they want equal time with their children, often what they're saying is, 'I want to be recognised as being just as good a parent as the other person.' I've also seen in parenting matters a parent seeking a specific time with their children during the week or the year, and more often than not this is because there's a particular event or sporting activity that they'd like to be involved in.

The minute I can understand why something is important to someone else, it makes it so much easier to formulate solutions that will work both for my client and for their former partner.

So how do you do this?

To be able to negotiate in a constructive way that will create outcomes that meet the needs of both you and your partner, you need to understand your goals and interests and, at the same time, understand theirs. This is not overly difficult but does take some time to just sit and think.

Go back to the activities you did earlier in this book. Go back to that perfect world in twelve months' time and imagine how it looks again. Some of how you'd like your life to look in twelve months' time will be particularly helpful for you in figuring out what you want to achieve as a part of your negotiation.

These goals are the answer to why you would like a particular outcome. They are, more often than not, intangible things. They're not an amount of money, a particular asset or an amount of time. They're our values – the things that are important to us.

When you're formulating a proposal or an offer to settle as part of your negotiation, if you can explain why you're proposing a particular outcome and if that explanation is grounded in an understanding of what's important to both of you, it makes it more and more difficult for that proposal to be argued against.

JULIE'S STORY

I was recently involved in a negotiation on behalf of a client called Julie, who's about forty years of age. She and her husband, Nick, had separated. He had been an entrepreneur throughout their marriage and ran a business that he had grown to provide them both with a reasonable income to support themselves. Julie was also employed and they did not have any children. Julie and Nick also had two investment properties, although neither of them wanted to live in those properties.

They had been negotiating for many months for Nick to keep one of the investment properties, Julie to keep the other and for Nick to keep his business. However, when the business was valued as a part of their legal process, some problems were unearthed. There were taxation difficulties associated with the business that neither of them had been aware of. This meant that Nick would be facing some financial challenges as he moved out of his divorce settlement.

While I wasn't acting for Nick, I expect that this caused him a lot of stress. Not only was he already negotiating a property settlement, he was now in a position where he may have had to repay monies to the Australian Tax Office that he had not counted on, simply due to an error that was not really his fault. This meant that when it came to negotiating his property settlement, Nick was adamant that those taxation debts should be included in our negotiations.

Julie had a different view. Julie and Nick had been separated for quite a few years by the time it came to negotiating their property settlement. Over that time Julie had had very limited involvement with his business, and Nick had had the benefit of all of the money that he was earning. In her mind, he had had the benefit of the money earned in his business and she had not, and therefore she didn't see why she should be responsible for monies that he may have to pay back to the Tax Office for that period.

Julie and Nick ultimately participated in mediation and, early in our negotiations at the mediation, we started to really analyse and understand what was important to each of them. For Julie, it was important that she retain one of the investment properties, as she saw that as her way of keeping a foot in the property market and ultimately rebuilding herself financially and moving forward.

Nick wanted to keep his business, but he was very anxious about potentially having to repay monies to the Tax Office in the future, and therefore was not interested in arrangements that would have him obtaining large amounts of finance to either retain the investment properties or pay money to Julie to divide their property.

After some negotiation, Julie proposed to Nick that she would keep both of their investment properties and pay him a sum of money to cover future issues that might arise with the Tax Office. This also meant that he didn't have to obtain finance to retain the investment properties. It was not a proposal that either Julie or Nick had thought about earlier that day. It was only because they both spent the time understanding each other's drivers and needs that this proposal could be made and was ultimately acceptable.

FINDING SETTLEMENT OPTIONS

One of the most enjoyable parts of my job as a family lawyer is negotiation. I do enjoy understanding why something is important to someone else and finding solutions that can meet the needs of two people who feel at odds with one another. I do this by trying to remain objective and looking at all the different options that might be available in any situation. When I'm thinking about those options I don't analyse them to consider whether they're going to be right, wrong or otherwise, or even achievable – I just start by creating options.

If we take the above example of Julie and Nick and think of their property settlement, here are several different settlement options:

1. Julie keeps one investment property, Nick keeps another plus his business, and an amount of money is exchanged to bring about the appropriate legal division of assets.
2. Nick keeps both the investment properties and his business and pays Julie an amount of money to bring about the appropriate legal division of assets.
3. One of the investment properties is sold, the proceeds are divided between Nick and Julie, the other investment property is kept by Julie and Nick keeps his business.
4. One of the investment properties is sold, the proceeds are divided between Nick and Julie, and the other investment property and the business are kept by Nick.
5. Both investment properties are sold, the money is divided between Nick and Julie and Nick keeps his business.
6. The business is sold, the investment properties are sold, the cash is realised and divided between Nick and Julie.
7. Julie keeps the business, Nick keeps the investment properties and there's a cash payment to bring about the appropriate legal division of assets.

And the list could go on and on...

These are seven options that could have been available to Nick and Julie in their circumstances. This is how I encourage you to start thinking when you're about to negotiate your settlement, whether it be financial or in relation to your children.

The moment that you can start to expand the range of available options for you and your partner, the easier your negotiation will become. I often will say to my clients, 'Give me the craziest thing you can think of here in terms of how we could solve this problem,' and from that question I often get some really great answers as to how their particular legal issue could be resolved. Often those answers are not outcomes that they would want, but the mere fact that their minds are able to turn to different solutions opens things up, and suddenly you can have constructive discussions about solutions that might work for both parties.

For both of you to walk away from your Family Law settlement and feel content that the outcome was appropriate, you will need to be looking for outcomes that are 'win win' or mutually beneficial. Chances are neither of you will achieve everything that you want, but as long as each of your main goals are met, an outcome can easily become mutually beneficial.

A FEW MORE TIPS FOR NEGOTIATION

If you are about to negotiate an outcome with your former partner, remember the following:

- **Your goals and values.** First of all, start by identifying what's actually important to both of you at the end of the day. These should be big picture, often intangible concepts. If the negotiation is in relation to your children, it might be that it is important that your children are educated in a particular way, that they are brought up to have certain values and beliefs, that they have stability across households, and that you're able to spend a significant amount of time with them that will enable you to be involved in their school activities, after-school activities, weekend and holiday time. Or if it's important for you that in the next few years you re-establish yourself in a home in an area in which you are used to living, then you may be negotiating to either retain the home that you and your former partner already own or perhaps to receive a sum of money that will enable you to ultimately purchase in the area you like. Do the same task for your spouse or, if you're on good speaking terms, ask them to do the same task and share your answers between you.

- **Be clear about what you want to achieve.** For example, if you are negotiating a property settlement with your former partner, be realistic but clear about the outcome you want. I have seen many separated couples become quickly entangled in complicated and expensive legal disputes because they are focused on negotiating over a percentage outcome. 'I want sixty per cent' versus 'I want sixty-five per cent'. The percentages are often immaterial and it is far more important to focus on the type and the value of the assets that you hope to receive at the end of the day.
- **Create options.** Once you have an understanding of your goals and the outcome you want to achieve, create some options that could potentially be solutions to your negotiation. If you're negotiating financial matters, sit and think about the different ways you could divide your property between you

and your spouse. If you are negotiating parenting matters, write a list of five to ten different ways that your parenting matters could be resolved. For example, if you would like an equal time arrangement with your children, think about all the different ways that an equal time arrangement could work. For example, it might be that each fortnight is divided into seven-night blocks between you and your partner. It might be that a week is divided. It might be that over the year, combining holiday time and time during the terms, there is some division of time between the two of you that ultimately amounts to an equal arrangement. There are lots of different ways that an equal time arrangement can be constructed. Try to come up with close to ten different ways that you could solve that problem.

- **Analyse the options.** Once you have all your options, sit and think about which ones are really going to meet both your needs and your partner's needs. If you can, start by trying to meet the needs of your partner before you meet your own needs. Once you've done that process, your list of ten options will probably come back to being two or three that might or might not work in your circumstances. They're the two or three that you might want to discuss with your partner to try to reach a resolution.
- **Avoid positional bargaining.** As much as you can, avoid negotiating for a position without having thought about whether that position ultimately meets your needs or your partner's needs. Look for proposals and outcomes that meet the needs of both of you, rather than simply proposing something that looks like the right number or the right division of time on paper.

- **Be careful where you put your flag in the sand.** A dear friend of mine uses this saying often during mediations when it comes to constructing a first offer. If you're in a constructive negotiation such as a mediation, there can be much fear and anticipation over who will put in the first offer. I think there is a sense that by putting in a first offer, you are somehow at a strategic disadvantage. I don't share that view and have learned that it's not whether you put in the first offer or not, it's how that offer is constructed and whether it is enticing that will determine how a negotiation will flow during the day.

  I call this 'where you put your flag in the sand'. Let's say that in a financial negotiation you have received legal advice that you might receive assets and money worth half a million dollars, but you decide to start your negotiation with an offer to receive $750,000. You could expect that your former partner will consider that an insulting offer, and will respond with an offer that is similarly insulting in that it is also a long way from a realistic outcome. If one person in a negotiation puts their 'flag in the sand' an awfully long way from a realistic outcome, the other person will often do the same in response and before you know it you have flags miles away from each other and often not enough time to bridge the gap.

  Avoid doing this as much as you can, and if you're in a situation where someone has already placed their flag a long way from a sensible outcome, you might be better placing your flag closer to a realistic outcome and holding your position rather than pitching them both far apart.

  It's common practice in the legal profession for opening proposals to be slightly unrealistic, and I often wonder whether this isn't counter intuitive. If you're in a constructive negotiation process, something like a mediation or collaborative practice, look only to proposals that are sensible, that meet the needs of both you and your partner and that are within the range of legal outcomes that you have been advised you will achieve, and try to avoid making offers or proposals that are simply designed to create room to negotiate. This will often just increase conflict, cost and delay in terms of resolving your legal issues.

- **Be the driver of your bus.** Whether you are negotiating on your own behalf or have a lawyer acting on your behalf or other advisers assisting you, I encourage you to be the driver of your own bus. Take advice as much as you can and understand the risks associated with not reaching an agreement. If you are negotiating financial matters, it is important to consider the financial cost that might be incurred if you were to take further legal steps, such as initiating Court proceedings. You should factor those into your decision making when it comes to making and receiving proposals for settlement. Similarly, in relation to parenting negotiations, it is important to take into account the financial costs, but also the costs to your family that could flow from lengthy and conflictual legal negotiations or Court proceedings. When it comes to your children, quality time with them is far more important than the number of hours or days in a week. Try to avoid getting fixated on numbers of nights and how they will be divided, and look instead at the quality of the time both of you can share with your children and what is best for them, depending on their ages and needs in life. Children are young for such a short period. It is important to remember that they will soon be adults and your relationship with them will continue well beyond the age of eighteen. Don't be afraid to give a little, to compromise, as certainty and an early outcome have benefits that are hard to understand unless you have yourself experienced a lengthy legal battle and spent thousands of dollars in the Court process.

- **Remember that there are many ways to be right.** There are so many different ways to solve any problem in life and many of them will be right. Don't be afraid, particularly when it comes to parenting matters, to try something, review it and then try something else. Children change over time and their needs and wishes will change. Your life and your partner's life will also change. It is often much easier to negotiate in small amounts of time, such as one or two years, rather than the next ten years. Don't be afraid to do this because if you can get some level of steady routine in place initially, chances are it will soon become much easier to discuss and change it as time goes by.
- **Always put yourself in the other person's shoes.** If you've been in a relationship with someone for a significant period of time, chances are you have a pretty good idea of how they think. Similarly they'll have a good understanding of how you think about most situations in life. When it comes to a negotiation, it's important that you try to think about how your proposals might be received by your former partner, particularly if you'd like them to be accepted. The more attractive you can make a proposal – in other words, the more you can make it meet the other person's needs – the greater chance you have of it being accepted.

By focusing on interest-based negotiation rather than positional bargaining and staying open to a range of settlement options, you and your partner will have a far greater chance of reaching a quick settlement that satisfies both of you.

If you want to go fast,

go alone.

If you want to go far,

go together.

AFRICAN PROVERB

Who can help?

YOUR ADVISORY TEAM

During a divorce or separation, there are a number of different advisers who can assist you with your separation. Of course I recommend you engage a family lawyer to advise you on the legal issues that are relevant to your family, but there are a range of other advisers who are just as important.

CHOOSING YOUR FAMILY LAWYER

Your lawyer – the shark?

I sense that there is a perception for many divorcing couples that when hiring a family lawyer they need to find someone who could perhaps be best described as a 'legal shark'. Historically and in the media, lawyers are often portrayed as cunning characters, obviously smart but not always with any sense of emotional understanding.

Finding the right family lawyer for you is perhaps similar to finding a doctor when you are suffering from ill health. You will be confiding in your family lawyer and sharing with them your innermost secrets, some of which you are unlikely to share with your family or friends. It is therefore essential that you find a lawyer with whom you feel comfortable having personal conversations.

In researching this book, I came across a particular divorce help book that included a chapter called Choosing Your Lawyer. An aptly named chapter; however, I was surprised to read the following statement: *'If there's an attorney known in town as the shark you are afraid your husband might use, consult the shark before he does.'*

A shark to me is a scary, cunning animal that has the propensity to chop off my arm next time I'm swimming in the ocean. Notably though, in my forty-eight years of swimming in the ocean I'm yet to lose a limb, so I guess the beauty of a shark is the fear his reputation for harm connotes without him actually having to cause any such harm.

Is the idea then to choose a person to act as a family lawyer who would create an atmosphere of fear with their mere presence lurking in the shadowy legal waters? I'm not sure that I would wish to confide in a shark-like person in any time of need. I like to think that the best family lawyers in our industry are anything but shark-like. They don't lurk in the shadows; they do anything but. They swim with their clients in the shallow waters, supporting them, sharing the load and guiding them down a well-chosen path. A great family lawyer is not going to chop off the limbs of either their client or a former spouse. Rather, they will find a way for both parties to a failed relationship to move forward into their new separate lives, with all of their limbs, dignity and hope intact. They do this by using skills that are anything but shark-like - skills like compassion, creativity, understanding and knowledge.

I encourage you to search for someone much more than a legal shark to guide you through your divorce - a time in your life when you will need much more than someone's limbs chopped off!

How to find your family lawyer

1. A referral from a close friend, colleague or trusted confidant will more often than not be a great place to start.
2. If you do not have the benefit of such a referral, it's time to start researching. Family lawyers can obtain a qualification in Australia denoting them as 'Accredited Specialists' in the area of Family Law. The legal world is ever changing, and gone are the days when lawyers could safely practise in every area of law. If your lawyer is still working in Family Law, personal injuries, property, commercial and every other form of law, it is unlikely that they can advise you as well as a practitioner who specialises in any one of those areas. Consequently, I would strongly recommend that you engage an Accredited Specialist in your state in the area of Family Law, as solicitors who have achieved this qualification have undertaken extensive study and assessment. This is a good first screening tool to identify a lawyer with expertise in this complicated area.

A list of all the Accredited Specialists in each state can be found by searching your local Law Society. The details of each of the Law Societies in each state are included in the Resources section of this book.

3. Once you have a shortlist of possible lawyers, it is time to do a bit more research. Sit and think about what sort of a lawyer you are looking for. For example, would you be more comfortable working with a male or a female? Or is that something that doesn't matter to you? Are you looking for an office that you can easily visit after hours or one that is close to your work? Would you like somewhere with a focus on a warm and friendly feeling or perhaps a larger corporate office? Would it help you to work with a lawyer that speaks a language you are more comfortable communicating in or has a deep understanding of a faith or culture you are connected to? Have a look at various lawyers' websites, which should give you a good indication of the type of law that the firm and lawyer is practising. Do their websites give you confidence that the firms are organised and up to date with their legal information? Is it important to you that you be able to communicate with your lawyer face-to-face or perhaps by email, Skype or other forms of communication? Ring the law firms on your shortlist and ask their administrative staff about the lawyers in their firm, their level of experience, their style of practice, how they charge and how they communicate with their clients.
4. If you are focused on keeping your family out of the Court process, ask the firm whether they undertake mediation, collaborative practice or other common forms of alternative dispute resolution as discussed in this book. While

most lawyers will tell you that they keep matters out of Court, this is not always the case. And if the firm is unable to provide you with information about those forms of dispute resolution, it is unlikely that they are focused on keeping your family out of the Court process. Therefore, don't be afraid to ask questions. Most firms will offer an initial appointment for clients at a reduced fee, often referred to as an initial consultation. Find out the cost of the appointment before attending, ask the administrative staff what information you should bring to the appointment, ensure that you know where the office is and where you can park, and allow plenty of time to get to the appointment.

5. If you are looking for a collaborative lawyer, search under the various state collaborative organisations listed in the Resources section of this book or the Australian Association of Collaborative Professionals website (www.collaborativeaustralia.com.au) for your local collaborative lawyers. A collaborative family lawyer needs to have undertaken further training to be accredited in this way. Ensure that your collaborative lawyer is qualified and registered with either their state or the international organisation.
6. If you are seeking the assistance of a mediator, again confirm that the mediator you are meeting with is qualified and registered with an appropriate body such as the Australian Mediation Association or similar state organisation. Ensure that your mediator is a family mediator. Mediation is now a regularly practised form of dispute resolution, and there are many different types of mediators available to assist you.

How to prepare for your first appointment with your lawyer

I've heard the first appointment between a client and a lawyer described as a bit like a first date. It's full of anticipation and nerves, and with the mutual hope of a long-lasting and successful relationship. In my experience, sometimes these appointments are easy and other times they can be quite difficult – for both the client and the lawyer!

When preparing to meet with your family lawyer for the first time, I recommend that you take a few moments to sit quietly and write a list of the questions that you hope to have answered in that initial appointment. This will ensure that when you attend your appointment, important things are not missed.

It is likely that your family lawyer will ask for basic information about you in your initial appointment. It is not expected that you provide a full chronology and detailed inventory of your relationship. Your first appointment with your lawyer should be more about you having any immediate and pressing questions answered, and ensuring that you can develop a rapport, confidence and trust in this lawyer.

Below is a checklist of information that you should consider preparing prior to your first appointment with your lawyer:

- Basic information about your family including your full names, your date of birth, your former partner's full name and date of birth, the names and dates of birth of any of the children of your relationship, the dates that your relationship began, that you married, that you separated and the date that your divorce was finalised.

- If you have property issues that need to be resolved, it can be helpful to bring with you a list of your assets, liabilities, superannuation and any other financial resources (something worth money).
- Information about your and your partner's income.
- Information about any assets, liabilities or superannuation you or your partner had when you first began to live together, and similarly any inheritances, significant financial gifts, large compensation payments (including personal injury and worker's compensation) or any other large sums of money that either of you received outside of your employment throughout the course of your relationship.
- If you have parenting issues to be resolved, it is likely that your lawyer will want to know about where the children are living at this time, any special needs they may have, their ages, routines, the schools they attend and your future plans for them, such as where they will go to school or whether there will be any change in the arrangements for where they are living or the time they are spending between you and your former spouse. Also write down a list of any specific concerns you have regarding the children. For example, you may want to go on a holiday and need information about what steps, if any, you should take.
- If you have any Court Orders in place or have previously engaged in any legal proceedings and have documents from other lawyers, it would be helpful to take copies of those documents with you to your first appointment.
- Information about you and your family, including culture and faith.
- Any concerns you have about risk or safety.

You might not have access to all this information and this will not be a problem in your appointment with your lawyer. Just gather what information you can. There is no need in an initial appointment to provide bundles of supporting documents. It is simpler for you to attend with a single sheet of bullet points.

It can be helpful to take a support person with you to your first appointment, as sometimes it can be overwhelming emotionally, but also the information can become confusing and it can be helpful to have another person there listening or even taking some notes on your behalf.

When you meet with your lawyer for the first time, ask them how they wish to communicate with you. If you have a preference as to how you wish to communicate with them, let them know. If you are a busy person, find out the most time- and cost-effective ways that you can work with them and suggest ways that they could work with you to ensure the easy exchange of information. Ask them how you can best help them to both save on your costs but also maximise the communication between the two of you. Ensure that you are clear on how they will charge you for work to be done. Also make sure you are clear on the 'next steps' they expect you to take to engage their office to assist you.

Do not expect to receive detailed advice from your lawyer in your first appointment regarding the exact outcome of your legal dispute. It is a bit like taking your car to the mechanic and asking them to tell you what is wrong without letting them open the bonnet. It is important that your lawyer takes the time to gather all the information necessary to provide you with accurate legal advice.

If, after this initial meeting, you are not entirely comfortable engaging them, then don't be afraid to do a bit more research and look for another lawyer. It is important to find the right lawyer for you and it is a lot easier to 'change' in the early stages than it will be when you are six months in and feeling like things are not really working between you.

WHO ELSE MIGHT I NEED?

While your family lawyer can assist you with the legal issues, there are a range of other issues that may arise for which you should consider obtaining expert advice.

Below are a list of common advisers that can assist throughout your separation, and an outline of the information and assistance they can provide.

Financial adviser

You may already have a financial adviser engaged to assist you. If not, this is a really good time to consider meeting with an adviser to help you set goals and plan your financial future.

Financial advisers can provide expert analysis of different settlement proposals and discuss with you how these options may meet both your short-term and long-term needs. This can be immensely helpful during your negotiation process as you can create a property division that will meet your goals and values.

After your separation, financial advisers can also be incredibly helpful in creating budgets and helping you set (and meet) goals for your financial future. Chances are, as a result of your separation, your financial circumstances have changed, and seeking the assistance of a professional to work out how you can still achieve the things that are important to you can be a really great way of helping you to keep focused on the big picture and agree on an early settlement.

How a financial adviser can help

'Separation is one of the most emotionally challenging and financially complex periods a person can experience. At a time when emotions are heightened and uncertainty is high, you are often required to make significant decisions that will shape your future – without always having a clear understanding of what life will look like financially on the other side. Many people enter this process feeling overwhelmed, anxious and unsure where to start. This is particularly common if you have not historically managed the household finances or been the primary financial decisionmaker, which can leave you feeling at an information disadvantage just when you need clarity most.

'We regularly see that the true cost of post-separation life is underestimated and that important decisions are made based on emotion rather than informed understanding. This can affect confidence in negotiations and make it harder to advocate for what you genuinely need. Our role is to help you step out of the emotional fog and into a clearer, calmer decision-making space. We do this by translating complex financial information into plain English and clear visuals, helping you understand how proposed settlements will impact both your short-term stability and your long-term wellbeing. We work with you to map out realistic living costs, align your lifestyle goals with numbers and explore "what if" scenarios so you can compare options with confidence.

'By providing reliable, negotiation-ready financial information, we support you to engage more constructively in discussions with your former partner and their advisers. This also allows your lawyer to focus on legal strategy and resolution, knowing that the financial foundations are sound. Throughout the process, we act as a financial sounding board, helping you sense-check decisions, understand trade-offs and feel supported as you move forward. The result is not just better financial outcomes, but a client who arrives at negotiations clearer, calmer and better prepared to advocate for a future that is sustainable, informed and right for them.'

Lynda McKie, Financial Adviser, Elston

Accountant

Chances are that you have an accountant involved in your financial affairs, particularly if you are a business person or business owner. Your accountant is an incredibly useful adviser during the divorce process. They will often have intimate knowledge of your business finances and personal finances, and can be a great neutral party to speak with both you and your spouse if you've both been engaging with them.

They will be able to explain how and why your affairs have been structured the way they have and assist in explaining how your business and investments have been performing. They can also help you identify your assets and liabilities and discuss different options for dividing them.

I will often work with my clients' accountants so we can share our knowledge and expertise to ensure that the financial outcomes after a divorce still meet their families' long-term strategies.

Accountants are also particularly useful in providing taxation advice if you have a business or a slightly complicated property or investment arrangement. There are taxation consequences that can flow from the division of assets upon a property settlement, and specific advice from your accountant before you enter into an agreement is essential.

The earlier you bring your accountant into the process, the more advice they may be able to provide to optimise the property division and the structure of your future affairs.

Bank or finance broker

It seems to be less and less common that we have relationships with our local bank manager but, if you do, this person can also be very helpful during your property settlement. I find most of my clients are working with financial advisers and brokers rather than the bank itself.

If you have assets such as a home or investment property, chances are at some point either you or your spouse is going to need to speak to your financier or bank about refinancing your home loan or obtaining further loans.

If you have a relationship with your local bank or a broker, it is good to speak with them early in the process about their requirements for finance and obtain information about what your finance limits are, particularly before you enter any negotiations. It's also a good opportunity to speak to a bank about any other products or assistance that they might be able to offer you, particularly if you need to establish new accounts.

> 'Separation is one of those times where getting clear, practical advice early can make a real difference. As a broker, my role is to help clients understand what's actually possible for them – whether that's refinancing to keep the home, accessing equity or setting themselves up to purchase again in the future.
>
> 'Often people come to me unsure about where they stand, particularly if their finances have been managed jointly. We can work through their income, assets and lending capacity in a straightforward way so they can make informed decisions before agreements are finalised.
>
> 'It's also about timing and understanding when you can act, what lenders will require, and how to structure things so the transition from joint to separate finances is as smooth as possible. Getting that clarity early can reduce stress and help avoid delays later in the settlement process.'
>
> **Justin Dickinson, BOQ, Mortgage Broker, Holo Online Mortgage Brokers**

Valuers

If you are trying to resolve a financial settlement after your divorce or separation, you may need to engage valuers to determine the value of some of the assets or even liabilities you and your partner have.

There are different types of valuers depending on the items you are trying to value.

The most common are real estate valuers (both residential and commercial), business valuers (who are usually highly specialised accountants) and other home contents / general property valuers (who will normally undertake valuations of things like motor vehicles, home contents, antiques or other specific items that you might have as a part of your property pool).

Real estate valuers. Real estate valuers are generally used to provide valuation advice on homes, investment properties or commercial properties. They are not real estate agents and are specialists who provide you with a written report on the value of your property. Generally, these valuers charge a fee for their valuation report. It is common now for separated couples to agree on a single valuer so that you are only obtaining one valuation report, rather than each of you obtaining separate reports.

A valuation will be a far more accurate reflection of the value of your property than a real estate appraisal, but sometimes real estate appraisals are a good place to commence negotiations. If you are going to be obtaining finance from a bank or other financial institution, chances are they will conduct a valuation of your property as part of your finance application. It can be helpful to have already obtained a good understanding of the value of your properties. This way you won't be surprised or disappointed if your financier conducts a valuation only to discover that what you thought your property was worth is quite different from a skilled professional's judgement.

Business valuers. It is a fine art to value a business in a Family Law matter, and something that you would have to run by your accountant, who would normally outsource this to another accountant who is a specialist in preparing valuations in these situations. Like the real estate valuers, usually one business valuer is engaged jointly by a couple to minimise cost and further dispute. It is important that you are both involved in the process of engaging the business valuer and receiving information about the value of the business. It is also important that they have access to all the documents they might need to assist them in valuing a business. These sorts of valuers are often also engaged to provide information and valuations on other corporate structures, including family trusts.

General property valuer. Depending on the items you need valued, there are a whole range of specialist valuers who can assist, and specialise in motor vehicles, caravans, boats, antique furniture and more. It can be a lot quicker and cheaper to jointly engage a valuer to have items valued rather than disputing what you think things may or may not be worth. This is particularly the case when it comes to home contents. While we often have home contents insurance that insures our possessions for over $100,000, it is rarely the case that the actual value of our home contents is anywhere close to that sum. While the insured value reflects the amount it might cost to replace all the items in your home, it is not the value of those items if you were to sell them today. For example, the last time I had a client undertake a valuation of their home contents, the contents of their four-bedroom home was valued between $6,000 and $7,000. This was considerably less than what the parties assumed and considerably less than what they had paid for those items. Home contents in particular are something that, as part of your final negotiation, you want to avoid placing any significant value on unless you have rare collections, antiques or other specific items of value. If you do have unusual or rare items, you should consider obtaining the assistance of a general property valuer.

Psychologists, social workers and other social scientists

There are many different services offered by social scientists, such as social workers, psychologists and counsellors, for people experiencing divorce and separation. These services include personal counselling, mediation, parenting programs, parenting advice and counselling for children, to name just a few.

It is well worth seeking assistance from social scientists during your separation or divorce, whether it is for you, for your family as a whole, or to seek assistance and advice in relation to your children.

> 'An experienced social scientist can offer great assistance in helping you work through the grief process and the negative emotions that you may be experiencing. They can help with reality checks and stop you from "catastrophising". In addition, there is a host of strategies that they can teach you to be as emotionally stable as possible through this difficult time.
>
> The same applies to your children. But a word of caution: it's fine to see someone and vent your feelings and express your point of view on your

relationship and what went wrong. But when it comes to kids, don't always assume that you are correct in knowing how they feel or what they think. They will say things to please you and sometimes that means they will bag their other parent to you and vice versa. Believing everything they say and then convincing a psychologist or social worker of it can be damaging. Some social scientists who are not experienced in this area can have difficulty remaining independent and balanced. They may not look at the evidence because they are too allied with you. Because of this, they can become biased if they are not working with both parents. This can end up in an almighty stoush when the other parent learns that the children are seeing someone who is not getting both sides of the story.'

Peter Jordan, Psychologist, Family Dispute Resolution Provider

General Practitioner

A good place to start if you don't have a direct referral to some of these services is your local doctor or GP. Your family doctor is often a great support during divorce and separation. They will themselves have an array of knowledge on the services available to help you and your partner through the difficult emotional side of your separation. They can also offer assistance through referrals for children who may need counselling and the like. If you feel that you are struggling emotionally, your GP is a good person to ask for assistance and direction, particularly if you might benefit from speaking with a psychologist or social worker.

'As a general practitioner I frequently see people undergoing the stress of relationship problems, separation and divorce. All GPs have training and experience in assessing and advising people with stress-related health conditions. Some GPs have completed additional training to provide formal psychological therapy whereas others can provide informal counselling. When appropriate, your GP will provide advice regarding the suitability of medication as well as facilitate referral to another health professional. Should you have any concerns regarding how your family is coping then making an appointment with your family's GP is a great start to get some help.'

Dr Paul Paterson, General Practitioner

School

Your children's school is often a great place to seek support and information during your divorce or separation. I don't mean that you should visit the school and personally seek support, but rather ask the school to keep an eye on your children and notify you of any changes in their behaviour. This can be a great way to ensure your kids are coping. Our children spend so much of their young lives at their school, and it is important that it is a safe haven where they are allowed to learn and grow. The school counsellors and chaplains are often great supports for your children during separation and divorce, and most schools will offer confidential counselling for children in these circumstances.

Church or other community social groups

Much support can be gained from local groups such as your church, your local community, sporting associations and the like. This is a great time to reconnect with your local community and form some bonds of support. Having things to do to keep you busy and keep your mind off things is a really important part of moving through your divorce process. Reach out to the people around you and seek their assistance to help you through this difficult time.

Friends and family

Finally, but perhaps most importantly, your friends and family will be a huge support during your divorce and separation. It is always important to keep in mind that our friends and family will do their best to support us, but they won't always be entirely independent in this situation. Be careful about the advice you receive from those closest to you. Try to ensure that financial and legal matters are kept separate and instead ask for emotional support from your friends and family during this difficult time. Having one or two trusted confidants is a great way of keeping you moving and focused on the bigger picture, particularly as you deal with the legal parts of your separation.

Every day is a new beginning.

UNKNOWN

Signing the paperwork!

By this stage the hard work should be done. You've negotiated your agreement, you've reached a resolution, but now it's time to formalise that and document it appropriately in a legal sense.

THE 3 TYPES OF LEGAL DOCUMENTS

All couples experiencing divorce and separation will end up with almost the same type of legal documents. There are three options:

1. **No documents at all.** In this case, couples use either a verbal agreement or an exchange of emails that sets out the terms under which they will deal with their parenting arrangements or financial matters.
2. **Informal documents.** One example of an informal document might be a signed agreement drafted by the couple containing the matters that are

important to them. Importantly, these documents rarely have any legal effect and can be more trouble than they are worth.

3. **Formal legally enforceable documents.** If you engage a family lawyer, they will assist you with the necessary legal documents that will set the terms for either the parenting of your children or the division of your finances. Generally the legal documents will be either Court Orders or Binding Agreements.

COURT ORDERS

A Court Order is a document sealed by the Family Law Courts. There are two types of Court Orders:

1. The first is called a 'Consent Order', meaning that the parties to the Order, or the couple, have both agreed to the terms of the Order. Once agreed, the Consent Order is drafted, signed and delivered to a Family Court for the Court to consider 'sealing' or making the Order. This is a procedural step and you will not need to attend Court for this to occur; rather your documents are posted or hand-delivered to the local Family Court where a Registrar considers their terms and then makes the Orders set out therein, presuming they comply with legal principles. It is not necessary for you to have the assistance of a lawyer to prepare or advise on a Consent Order, although it is recommended. Around ninety per cent of the families I assist in my role as a family lawyer end up with a Consent Order detailing their parenting arrangements or financial settlements.

2. The second type of Court Order is made by a Judge at the end of a Court hearing or trial. In this scenario the couple involved have not agreed to the terms of their Order and have sought the assistance of a Judge to determine either their parenting or financial matters. In the worst cases I have had clients wait some three or more years to achieve a final Court Order and spend the equivalent of a small house in legal fees to obtain the very same document that can be obtained by agreement. If you are asking the Court to make an Order you will have limited control over the terms of that Order. You will also have limited control over the time it might take to obtain that Order and the legal costs involved. However, only a very small percentage of separating families find their way to the end of the Court process and require a Judge to make a decision, so the odds are in your favour!

BINDING AGREEMENTS

The second type of formal legal document is in essence a contract between you as a couple. This contract, when drafted correctly, is binding on you both. There are different types of Binding Agreements that can be made, including agreements relating to your children, agreements relating to financial matters, and agreements relating to child support.

Binding Agreements relating to your children

You can document agreements relating to your children in a Parenting Plan, or a document signed by both parents that contains matters relating to the parenting of your children. A Parenting Plan is not enforceable in the way that a Court Order can be. However, a Parenting Plan has significant legal effect and must be considered by a Family Court if that Court is later asked to make parenting Orders.

Binding Agreements relating to your finances

For financial matters such as the division of your property or splitting of your income (spouse maintenance), you can use a Binding Financial Agreement. This is a binding contract between you and your spouse. These types of agreements are most commonly used for 'pre-nuptial agreements' but they can also be used at the end of a marriage or de facto relationship to document the division of assets and income. Binding Financial Agreements are often used by couples who are considering a division of their finances in a way that might be 'creative'. As a general principle, the Family Courts prefer to see couples ending their financial ties and moving on. Some couples prefer to keep assets together for a period of time after a relationship breakdown. This has become more common in recent years due to the poor economic performance of many investments and the downturn in the property market. Binding Financial Agreements can also be used where a couple is seeking to divide their finances in a way that is outside what a Family Court would consider appropriate in the circumstances of that case. Binding Financial Agreements are a helpful tool in many settlements; however, you and your former partner must both have received independent legal advice on the terms for them to be binding. As such, they are not a document you could properly prepare and finalise without the assistance of lawyers.

Binding Agreements relating to child support

Another form of agreement that is commonly used by parents is a Child Support Agreement. This is a contract between parents setting out how they might manage the financial aspects of raising children. There are two types of Child Support Agreements - a limited agreement and a binding agreement. A limited agreement offers flexibility for parents who don't want to commit to long-term agreements. Parents do not need to have had legal advice to enter into this type of Child Support Agreement and they are reasonably easy to terminate by either parent if circumstances change. A Binding Child Support Agreement, however, will bind parents for the term of the agreement, generally until the children reach the age of eighteen years. Parents wishing to enter into a Binding Child Support Agreement will need independent legal advice about their agreement before it is signed.

Binding Agreements are used by some couples instead of a Consent Order when they don't want the formality of a Court Order, or when they want to ensure privacy by not lodging documents with the Courts. Another advantage of Binding Agreements is that they can offer significant flexibility as to what can be included. By contrast, for a Court Order to issue, its terms must meet the relevant legal principles.

SO WHICH DOCUMENTS DO I NEED?

There is no 'one-size-fits-all' document. Every family is unique and therefore every settlement document will be in its own way different, so do seek specific legal advice to determine which type of document might be best for you.

The majority of clients I work with are seeking a combination of these legal documents. The most common would be a Consent Order, which contains terms dividing their finances and also setting out their parenting arrangements. Binding Financial Agreements are less commonly used and Binding Child Support Agreements suit parents who wish to move away from the standard formula applied by the Department of Human Services.

You can also mix and match. For example, you might have a Consent Order for your financial affairs, a Parenting Plan for you parenting arrangements and a Binding Child Support Agreement for the financial matters relating to your children. Alternatively you might just need a Parenting Plan into which you could include terms for the financial arrangements for your children by way of a Limited Child Support Agreement.

When you are considering your financial matters I strongly recommend that you obtain a Consent Order or Binding Financial Agreement, as there can be significant disadvantages if you don't properly end your financial relationship. Further, these documents, when prepared properly, will enable the transfer of significant assets such as your home or other investments without incurring taxes such as stamp duty and capital gains tax.

SHOULD YOU GET YOUR LAWYER INVOLVED?

If you've managed to do all the hard work yourselves and have reached an agreement - and this is a great thing - don't be afraid to take that agreement to lawyers to seek advice on how to draft it up. This will save you a lot of time and money as it is very difficult to appropriately draft Consent Orders and have them lodged with the Courts.

You may find, upon meeting with lawyers, that they identify some other advantages and disadvantages to the agreement that you and your spouse reached. I know that, for some clients, there is a fear that if they take their agreement to a lawyer it will somehow be undone. This should not be the case, but it is our job to advise you and highlight any pitfalls of any agreements you've reached. It's better to have this information before you proceed and finalise things so that it can be rectified, and it just means that you and your partner might need to sit down and think again about the terms of your agreement.

It's also important to keep in mind, particularly when it comes to financial matters, that an agreement that you and your spouse have reached in relation to the division of your property is not legally binding until it is turned into either a Consent Order and filed with the Family Courts, or drafted into a Binding Financial Agreement, which again is a specific legal contract for which you will need assistance from lawyers.

CAN I CHANGE MY AGREEMENT?

Once you have a legally binding document such as a Consent Order or Binding Financial Agreement, it can become difficult to change. The word 'binding' in a legal sense will generally mean that you and your spouse are committed to the terms of the document and it will be very hard to get out of it. All Court Orders are 'binding' and there can be very serious consequences that flow if you do not comply with the terms of a Court Order. Similarly, a Binding Financial Agreement or Binding Child Support Agreement should be seen as being like a Court Order in that you will be required to comply with their terms. It is because of the significant consequences that flow from these types of documents that you will be required to have independent legal advice as to their effect before you sign off on them.

There are some differences here, though, between financial and parenting matters. There is a level of legal understanding that as children grow they change and, as such, their parenting arrangements may need to change. For this reason, having a Parenting Plan that offers a level of flexibility can be a great way of ensuring that you and your partner can continue to sit down and review arrangements for your children as they get older . You will not need the specific assistance of lawyers to do this if you are able to reach an agreement on your own.

WHAT IF I NEED TO CHANGE A COURT ORDER?

If you have a Court Order in place in relation to your children, this cannot be varied or changed without the agreement of both of you or without a further Court Order. It is not as simple as just walking back into a Family Court a few years down the track and saying something like, 'This hasn't worked and I want to change it.' There needs to be good reason and you need to be able to establish that there is some benefit to your children in having those arrangements changed. If you have a Court Order in place for your children, you should work on the basis that it is in place until the children turn eighteen, unless something quite significant changes in their lives.

When it comes to your financial matters, whether you have a Court Order or a Binding Financial Agreement, it would be very difficult to change that once the Agreement or Order has been finalised. You should work on the basis that, once that document is finalised, it is finished. It is really only in circumstances where you can establish that something was not known – perhaps one of you didn't properly advise the other of all the relevant information at that time, or there was some level of duress or inappropriate behaviour – that those Agreements or Orders could perhaps be revisited at a later point.

If you and your spouse are in agreement that a financial arrangement needs to be changed, that is a slightly different situation, and it potentially could be revisited, but you would need to obtain specific advice from a specialist family lawyer.

In short, once formal agreements are reached, you need to work on the basis that they are in place and enforceable and you should try to stick to them as much as possible.

PART 4

Moving On

Don't cry over the past,

it's gone.

Don't stress about the future,

it hasn't arrived.

Live in the present

and make it beautiful.

UNKNOWN

Moving on

It is very easy to bring an end to the legal issues arising from your separation or divorce through a series of formal documents. But the emotional impact may take a significant amount of time to pass.

However, you don't want your divorce or your separation to become a devastating part of your life where you remain stuck. Rather, you want to be able to look back on it as an experience that you are perhaps very sad about, but that you and your partner managed well. This is by no means easy, but things will get easier – one day you will wake up in the morning and everything will just feel better.

I find in working with separating couples that there is almost an anti-climax when the divorce is granted or the legal process comes to an end. The legal side of your separation can go on for some time and is all consuming, and then suddenly it comes to an end. It is at this time that I find my clients are faced with the reality of their situation, whether that is good or bad.

At this time, it's important to take care of yourself, along with communicating compassionately with your former partner and remaining flexible – these traits will help with the practicalities that come up after your separation.

TAKING CARE OF YOURSELF

Don't expect too much of yourself at this time. Allow yourself time to grieve and move forward. Set small achievable goals and focus on the bigger picture and the future. I like to focus on the silver linings. They can be very hard to find, particularly when things are really tough, but if you can find even the simplest and smallest silver lining in any difficult situation, it will make it so much easier to start to move on and move forward.

When speaking to my clients and friends about what they did to move forward after their divorces and separations, almost all of them spoke about the need to remain positive, keep looking forward, set small achievable goals and try a few new things. Perhaps the most important thing that I can suggest is that you do try to maintain a positive attitude. No matter how difficult things become, find those silver linings and focus on them. They will pull you through this really difficult time.

That said, no matter how much you try to stay positive, you may need to seek some professional assistance to help you move forward.

THE IMPORTANCE OF CONTINUING COMMUNICATION AND COMPASSION

Even after you have finalised legal issues, particularly when it comes to parenting matters, there's a chance that you'll still find some bumps along the road as your life moves forward. As much as possible, try to keep communication between yourself and your former partner open. No matter how frustrated you become with their behaviour, if you can keep communication channels alive, it will make things a lot easier for both of you.

In my experience, once the legal process comes to an end, communication tends to improve over time. I appreciate that not everyone will want to sit down every other week with their ex-partner over coffee, but you will be able to communicate in a civil and businesslike manner.

Try to remember my other favourite saying: 'Let a few goals go through to the keeper.' Don't feel the need to respond to every comment, email or text message. Just because something is said, does not make it true. Pick the things that really matter to you and your children – they're the ones to focus on and, other than that, try to avoid arguments wherever you can.

TRY TO BE FLEXIBLE

Even where Orders have been put in place that are very specific and provide for time for your children between both of you, there will always be occasions when something comes up that hasn't been covered by those Orders.

A common example of this is important family events such as weddings, significant birthdays and sometimes even funerals. Those are times when it is so important that you and your former partner are able to have a conversation and perhaps come up with an arrangement for your children that might be different from what you subscribed to in your Agreement or through a Court Order.

I advise my clients to pick their battles wisely. In other words, try to be flexible on some of these things because it's only a matter of time before you will be asking for the same level of flexibility in response. Of course, there's no guarantee that it will be given to you, but there's a much greater chance, if you've allowed a level of flexibility for your former partner, that they will consider it when you ask for the same in return.

A FEW PRACTICALITIES TO THINK ABOUT AFTER YOUR SEPARATION

Can I change my name?

You are free to keep your married name or change it after your divorce. If you wish to change it you should contact the Registry of Births, Deaths and Marriages in your state and they will guide you through the process. You previously had to make an application to the Courts by way of deed poll, but that is no longer necessary.

While the process is relatively straightforward, it can be time consuming when it comes to changing bank accounts and other things (if you changed your name when you married you will have some idea of what's involved).

Can I change my children's surname?

When it comes to your children, it is not as simple as changing their name through a form. If you and your partner agree, you can change the surname of your children, but if you don't agree you would need to make an application to the Family Courts to seek a decision regarding their name.

Don't forget your Will

A divorce can have a significant impact on any Will that you obtained during your marriage. In essence, a divorce will render a Will, insofar as it relates to your former partner, void unless that Will was made in contemplation of your divorce. It is important that at the point of your separation or divorce you consider updating your Will, or perhaps even starting afresh.

It is a good time to do a stocktake of all your financial and personal affairs and just see what might need to be updated, given that your circumstances have changed. Superannuation funds and insurance policies are one area where you will have to consider your nominated beneficiaries within those funds and policies.

New partners - introducing them to the children

This is not a legal issue, and you cannot stop a parent and their new partner from spending time with your children (unless that partner poses some risk to your children); however, it can be a point that leads to conflict, even when the separation occurred many years before. If you have formed a new significant relationship, particularly if you have children, it is always best to try to inform your former partner of your new relationship rather than have them hear about it from your children after a weekend visit. Conversely, if your children return home to speak about their mother or father's new partner, try not to take out your concern or frustration on them and avoid questioning them extensively.

I've seen people deal with this issue in many different ways. Sometimes the new partner is introduced to the old partner to take away that element of fear of the unknown. Other times it simply doesn't matter. I have, however, seen the introduction of a new partner trigger extensive conflict and, at times, litigation, and I encourage you to do all you can to avoid this.

If you are considering introducing a new partner to your children, then do take your time in doing this. Focus on how your children might feel about this and remind them at all times that their mother and father remain their mother and father, no matter who else is in their lives.

I heard a client recently describe how he had explained the role of his new girlfriend to his children. He explained to them that their mother was still their mother and he was still their father and nothing would ever change that. He also explained that his new partner cared about them just like many other people did in their lives – their aunts, their uncles, their cousins, their grandparents and other close family friends. This is a good way to enable children to understand that there are many adults in their lives, all of whom care about them, and that that is a good thing, not a bad thing.

There is no right or wrong way to deal with this tricky issue, but try to think about it from the perspective of your children and your former partner. If it is only two or three weeks after your marriage has broken down, then do think very carefully before introducing a new partner to either your former partner or your children. You can expect that that will cause considerable conflict, which will probably slow down the resolution of your larger legal issues.

Now that we've separated, I'd like to move

After a divorce or separation, either one or both of you will likely have to find alternative accommodation. This is not a difficulty if you are both still living in the same area, but can become a significant difficulty in circumstances where one partner wants to move a long distance away, for example interstate or to another town, particularly when it might affect children.

When children are involved, it is important that you speak to your partner before trying to move a long distance that would affect the capacity of your children to spend time with each of you. If you move without first having discussed it and reached some agreement, there can be significant legal consequences. It is common, particularly in Australia, for people to move between states and towns, certainly when it comes to changes of work. It's not that you won't be able to move, it's just that there is an appropriate process that should be followed to enable this to occur. At the end of the day, your focus should be on how you can ensure that your children are best able to have a relationship with both of their parents, no matter where you both are living.

There are several ways you can move on from your separation and focus on your future. Just keep in mind that some of these, particularly if you have children, will affect your former spouse, and the best way to ensure you both get what you want and are able to maintain a peaceful relationship is by keeping your former spouse informed of any major changes you are considering, and continuing to treat them with respect.

New beginnings
are often disguised
as painful
endings.

LAO TZU

Conclusion

NEW BEGINNINGS

If you've made it to the end of this book, then hopefully you are ready to start creating better things and new beginnings. None of us knows what is around the corner in life, but I like to think that it is full of surprises – surprises that are more often good than bad.

Your separation and divorce can have a significant impact on you, your family, your friends and others around you. Learn from this experience and don't let it affect the rest of your life. Use it as a time for change – positive change. Allow yourself to do what you want to do – things that you may not have been able to do when you were married or in that relationship. Maybe it's time to paint a wall at home hot pink. Maybe it's time to find that chair that you always wanted. Maybe it's time to join a new club, play a sport or join the gym. It might be time to get back into the workforce, or change your role in the workforce.

Just do something – something that signifies change, something that's positive, something that's important to you and something that is just for you. Whatever it is, now is a great opportunity for you to start creating the life that you want to live in the future.

I do wish you and your family all the best on this difficult journey and I hope that, as you find your way through the legal issues and your divorce, you are able to find many silver linings. Just because your past didn't turn out the way you wanted it to, doesn't mean that your future can't be better than you imagined.

When life gives you lemons, make a margarita!

Acknowledgements

I first wrote *Splitsville* when I was thirty-six years of age. I had recently become a mum for the first time and had been working as a family lawyer for sixteen years. Fast forward to 2026 – I am older and, I like to think, wiser. I still enjoy the work I do as a family lawyer and consider it a great privilege to stand beside so many extraordinary people at such challenging times in their lives.

When I set out to write *Splitsville* I wanted to create a resource that I could give to a friend that would help them to learn all the things I have come to see in my work before they embark on the process.

I hope this book becomes a bit of a guide for you as you navigate this chapter of your life too.

Who knows, there might be a third edition if our Family Laws keep changing the way they have this past decade.

Splitsville was many years in my mind and now finally is here (twice) in the making. I would like to thank the many people who have supported me on this journey.

In particular, I would like to thank my friends, family and colleagues who have put up with endless questions, note-taking during our conversations and weekend trips interrupted by my musings on divorce and separation.

To my two Melissas – one eternally in my heart and the other here with me always, thank you for your ongoing support as my closest friends and for putting up with the whirlwind that is the mind of Clarissa.

To my team at Brisbane Family Law Centre in your many iterations – thank you for inspiring me every day to find new ways to help Australian families.

To my colleagues Jen, Rob, Colin, Ann and John – the years of mentorship have been invaluable and no doubt you will find many of the ideas in this book have stemmed from lessons you have taught me.

And perhaps most importantly, thank you to my parents, Jane and Forster, my husband, Oliver, and my daughters London and Daisy, who teach me every single day the value of my life and remind me of just how important relationships are to all of us.

The author's story

Clarissa Rayward practises as a Divorce Lawyer and mediator in Brisbane, Queensland, Australia, where she is the Director of the boutique specialist Family Law firm, Brisbane Family Law Centre, and the mediation practice, Brisbane Family Mediation Centre.

Often known as The Happy Family Lawyer, Clarissa has built her career around changing the way Australian families experience separation and divorce – by rethinking the way Family Law is practised. Her work focuses on helping families navigate separation with dignity, clarity and care while minimising the emotional and financial costs that often come with the traditional Court-based process.

With more than twenty-five years' experience in the legal industry, Clarissa has seen firsthand the profound impact separation can have on parents and children alike. This experience has shaped her commitment to keeping families out of the Family Courts wherever possible, and to supporting cooperative, informed and child-focused outcomes.

Alongside her work with families, Clarissa is deeply committed to supporting the wellbeing and sustainability of those who work in the legal profession. She is the author of *Happy Lawyer Happy Life*, a book and platform dedicated to improving lawyer wellbeing and reshaping legal practice through connection, community and innovation. Through her writing, podcasting, coaching programs and speaking engagements, Clarissa works with lawyers across Australia to help them build healthier, more values-aligned careers – believing that when lawyers are well supported, families are better served.

Clarissa is a mother, wife, sister, daughter and friend and believes that her relationships with those around her are the most valuable part of her life. She is passionate about families and passionate about her work as a family lawyer and hopes to be known for changing the way Australian families experience separation and divorce for the better.

You can contact Clarissa at her practice, Brisbane Family Law Centre:

P: (+61) 73862 1955

E: clarissa@bflc.com.au

W: www.bflc.com.au

www.brisbanefamilymediationcentre.com.au

Helpful Resources

HERE IS A LIST OF HELPFUL ORGANISATIONS AND RESOURCES THAT CAN OFFER ASSISTANCE WITH YOUR SEPARATION OR DIVORCE

Government resources

FAMILY RELATIONSHIPS ONLINE

www.familyrelationships.gov.au

Information about family relationship services, separation, parenting arrangements and referrals to local support services.

SERVICES AUSTRALIA

www.humanservices.gov.au/breaking-up-with-your-partner

Provides information about child support, family assistance payments and other government financial support.

FEDERAL REGISTRAR OF LEGISLATION

www.comlaw.gov.au

Access to current Commonwealth legislation, including the Family Law Act.

AUSTRALASIAN LEGAL INFORMATION INSTITUTE (AUSTLII)

www.austlii.edu.au

Free access to legislation, case law and legal materials.

Counselling and emotional support

The following organisations provide support and counselling services:

LIFELINE AUSTRALIA
www.lifeline.org.au

BEYOND BLUE
www.beyondblue.org.au

Support for anxiety, depression and mental health challenges.

REACHOUT
www.au.reachout.com

Support and resources for young people and parents.

KIDS HELPLINE
www.kidshelpline.com.au

Free, confidential counselling for children and young people aged 5–25.

RELATIONSHIPS AUSTRALIA
www.relationships.org.au

MENSLINE AUSTRALIA

www.mensline.org.au

Telephone and online counselling support for men and their families.

Legal services

NATIONAL ASSOCIATION OF COMMUNITY LEGAL CENTRES

If you are seeking free legal advice, you can find the contact details for a community legal centre near to you here:

www.clcs.org.au/legal-help/

LEGAL AID SERVICES

In almost all States and Territories you will find a Legal Aid service that may be able to offer legal advice and representation at no cost or a reduced cost. For the contact details of the Legal Aid Office in your area, visit:

www.australia.gov.au/content/legal-aid

Law societies in Australia

The Law Societies in each state can assist with referrals to specialist family lawyers.

QUEENSLAND LAW SOCIETY
www.qls.com.au

LAW SOCIETY OF NEW SOUTH WALES
www.lawsociety.com.au

LAW INSTITUTE VICTORIA
www.liv.asn.au

LAW SOCIETY OF SOUTH AUSTRALIA
www.lawsocietysa.asn.au

LAW SOCIETY OF WESTERN AUSTRALIA
www.lawsocietywa.asn.au

LAW SOCIETY OF TASMANIA
www.lst.org.au

LAW SOCIETY OF THE AUSTRALIAN CAPITAL TERRITORY
www.actlawsociety.asn.au

LAW SOCIETY NORTHERN TERRITORY
www.lawsocietynt.asn.au

Collaborative law

The following organisations can assist with more information about the Collaborative Law Process:

AUSTRALIAN ASSOCIATION OF COLLABORATIVE PROFESSIONALS

www.collaborativepractice.com

Mediation

For further information about mediation and to find Accredited Mediators or Family Dispute Resolution providers, visit:

FAMILY RELATIONSHIP CENTRES

www.familyrelationships.gov.au/find-local-help

LIST OF REGISTERED FAMILY DISPUTE RESOLUTION PROVIDERS NATIONWIDE

www.fdrr.ag.gov.au/fdrr

AUSTRALIAN MEDIATION ASSOCIATION

www.ama.asn.au

RESOLUTION INSTITUTE

www.resolution.institute

AUSTRALIAN INSTITUTE OF FAMILY STUDIES

www.aifs.gov.au

Courts

The following websites provide further information about the Family Courts in Australia.

FAMILY LAW COURTS
www.fcfcoa.gov.au

COMMONWEALTH COURTS PORTAL (FOR FILING COURT DOCUMENTS)
www.comcourts.gov.au

Your Separation Toolkit

Here you will find practical tools to help you take the next steps with confidence.

Separation comes with a lot of moving parts – legal, financial and emotional. It can feel overwhelming to hold it all in your head. That's why we've created this Toolkit: a set of simple, step-by-step checklists and worksheets designed to make the process clearer and more manageable.

These tools are here to:

- Give you structure when things feel uncertain
- Help you prepare for legal advice and mediation
- Save time and costs by keeping your information organised
- Free up headspace so you can focus on what matters most – yourself and your children

WHAT'S INSIDE

- ✓ First 30 Days Checklist – the urgent steps to take straight after separation
- ✓ Digital Separation Checklist – keep your online life secure and private
- ✓ Property Pool Checklist – helping you to identify your wealth
- ✓ Property Pool Worksheet – list what you own and what you owe
- ✓ Parenting Information Checklist – keep your children's details and routines in one place
- ✓ Family Safety Checklist

HOW TO USE THIS TOOLKIT

You don't need to complete every box perfectly or all at once. Start where you can, use the checklists as prompts, and bring what you have to your appointments. Even partial notes will give your advisers a clearer picture and help them give you better advice.

This Toolkit is here to support you, not to add pressure. Use it in the way that feels most helpful – and remember, each small step forward is progress.

First 30 days after separation checklist

The first month after separation can feel overwhelming – there's often so much to think about, and it's hard to know what to tackle first. This checklist is designed to help you focus on the most important legal and practical steps, alongside caring for yourself and your children. You don't need to tick off everything straight away – start with the urgent tasks, then work through the rest at your own pace. Each small step you take will make things a little clearer and help you feel more in control.

SAFETY & IMMEDIATE NEEDS

- ☐ Make sure you and your children are safe
- ☐ If needed, update locks, security or safety plans
- ☐ Seek urgent support if family violence is a concern (police, DV services)

LEGAL & PRACTICAL STEPS

- ☐ Book an initial consultation with a family lawyer
- ☐ Gather key documents (ID, bank statements, payslips, property details, superannuation, children's records)
- ☐ Note any urgent deadlines (e.g. mortgage payments, rent, bills)
- ☐ Open a new bank account in your name only (if needed)
- ☐ Update Centrelink, Medicare, MyGov or child support details if circumstances have changed

FINANCIAL ORGANISATION

- ☐ List all assets, debts and liabilities (shared & individual)
- ☐ Check whose name is on household bills, loans, insurance policies
- ☐ Review income and expenses – create a basic budget for the next few months

PARENTING ARRANGEMENTS

- ☐ Confirm immediate care routines for children (who, when, where)
- ☐ Share key information (school, medical, activities) with the other parent
- ☐ Keep communication respectful and practical (consider a co-parenting app)
- ☐ Focus on stability for children – keep school, friends and routines consistent where possible

EMOTIONAL & SUPPORTIVE STEPS

- ☐ Tell one or two trusted friends / family members what's happening
- ☐ Book time with a counsellor or GP if you need support
- ☐ Allow yourself time to rest – separation is stressful, even when it's amicable
- ☐ Start a private journal or notes file to record important events and reflections

Remember, you don't have to do all of this on your own. Separation is a big change, and it's normal to need support along the way. Reach out to trusted friends, family or professionals when you need help. Taking these steps one at a time, with the right guidance, will give you a stronger foundation as you move forward.

Property pool quick checklist

This Checklist is designed to help you start to identify the types of assets, liabilities and superannuation that make up your property pool – this is information your lawyer or mediator will ultimately need. You don't need everything perfectly gathered before seeking advice – even starting with a few key items will help your advisers guide you more effectively

REAL ESTATE

- ☐ Family home
- ☐ Investment property(ies)
- ☐ Other land

VEHICLES & PERSONAL PROPERTY

- ☐ Car(s) / motorbike(s)
- ☐ Furniture / household contents
- ☐ Jewellery, art or collectibles
- ☐ Other valuable items

BANK ACCOUNTS & INVESTMENTS

- ☐ Everyday bank accounts
- ☐ Savings accounts
- ☐ Shares / managed funds
- ☐ Term deposits / other investments

SUPERANNUATION

- ☐ My super fund(s) - member statements available
- ☐ Partner's super fund(s) - member statements available

BUSINESSES & TRUSTS

- ☐ Business ownership / directorships
- ☐ Trust interests (family trust, unit trust, etc.)
- ☐ Company shares

LIABILITIES (WHAT YOU OWE)

- ☐ Mortgage(s)
- ☐ Personal loan(s)
- ☐ Credit card(s)
- ☐ Car loan(s) / lease(s)
- ☐ Tax debt(s)
- ☐ Other debts

NOTES FOR YOU

- Don't worry if you don't know the values yet - ticking the boxes helps identify what information is needed.
- Collect statements, contracts or documents for each item where you can.
- Bring this checklist (even partly completed) to your lawyer - it will save time and help focus the advice you receive.

Property pool worksheet

This worksheet is to help you start to collate a clear picture of your financial position - often called the property pool.

List everything you and your former partner own (assets) and everything you owe (liabilities). Exact figures aren't essential at this stage; estimates are fine.

REAL ESTATE			
PROPERTY	**IN WHOSE NAME?**	**VALUE ($)**	**NOTES** Address, mortgage details, valuation obtained / estimated
Family home			
Investment property(ies)			
Other land			

VEHICLES & PERSONAL PROPERTY			
ITEM	**IN WHOSE NAME?**	**VALUE ($)**	**NOTES**
Car(s) / motorbike(s)			
Furniture / household contents			
Jewellery / art / collectibles			
Other			

BANK ACCOUNTS & INVESTMENTS			
ACCOUNT / INVESTMENT	**IN WHOSE NAME?**	**BALANCE / VALUE ($)**	**NOTES** Bank, account no., type of investment
Everyday accounts			
Savings accounts			
Shares / managed funds			
Term deposits			

SUPERANNUATION			
FUND NAME	**MEMBER NAME**	**BALANCE ($)**	**NOTES** Member no., insurance included, defined benefit / accumulation
Super Fund 1			
Super Fund 2			

BUSINESSES & TRUSTS			
BUSINESS / TRUST NAME	**OWNERSHIP** e.g., % or trustee	**VALUE ($)**	**NOTES** ABN, company structure, accountant contact
Business 1			
Business 2			

LIABILITIES (WHAT YOU OWE)			
LIABILITY	**IN WHOSE NAME?**	**AMOUNT OWING ($)**	**NOTES**
Mortgage(s)			
Personal loan(s)			
Credit card(s)			
Car loan(s) / lease(s)			
Tax debt(s)			
Other			

TOTAL SUMMARY	
Total Assets	$
Total Liabilities	$
Net Property Pool (Assets-Liabilities)	**$**

Tip: Bring this worksheet – even partly filled – to your meetings with any advisers. It will save time, reduce stress, and help your lawyer give clearer advice.

Parenting information checklist

This checklist is designed to help gather information that will be needed by your lawyer or mediator in relation to your children.

CHILDREN'S DETAILS

- ☐ Full names and dates of birth
- ☐ Birth certificates
- ☐ Current addresses

CARE ARRANGEMENTS

- ☐ Current weekly routine (who the children live with, changeover times)
- ☐ School / daycare drop-off and pick-up details
- ☐ Upcoming holidays or special occasions to plan for

EDUCATION

- ☐ School enrolment details
- ☐ Recent school reports
- ☐ Details of any learning or educational supports
- ☐ Notes on extra-curricular activities (sport, music, dance, etc.)

HEALTH

- ☐ Summary of any health needs
- ☐ Details of any treating medical professionals
- ☐ Any medication or other treatment plans
- ☐ Any relevant medical or professional reports

SUPPORT & SPECIAL NEEDS

- ☐ Notes on learning needs, diagnoses or extra support at school
- ☐ NDIS plan details (if applicable)

OTHER IMPORTANT INFORMATION

- ☐ Religious or cultural considerations
- ☐ Extended family or support people involved in care
- ☐ Children's passports (if applicable)

NOTES FOR YOU

- Don't stress if you don't have everything ready – even a partial list is a good start.
- Written routines and records help make care arrangements smoother and clearer for everyone.
- Bringing this to your lawyer or mediator will help ensure any agreements reflect your children's real needs.

Tip: Keep copies of key documents (like birth certificates, school reports, medical info) in one folder – digital or paper – so you can share them easily if required.

Digital separation checklist

Separation isn't only about houses, cars and bank accounts – your digital life matters too. Protecting online accounts, devices and information can prevent stress, protect your privacy, and keep things safe for you and your children. Here is a checklist to help you consider any changes you might need to make.

SECURE YOUR DEVICES

☐ Change passcodes on phone and tablet

☐ Update passwords on computer(s)

☐ Turn off shared Apple IDs / Google accounts

☐ Review apps with location sharing or family tracking

PROTECT YOUR ONLINE ACCOUNTS

☐ Update personal email password

☐ Turn on two-factor authentication

☐ Change passwords for social media (Facebook, Instagram, LinkedIn)

☐ Change passwords for banking and PayPal

☐ Update MyGov and Centrelink login

☐ Secure cloud storage (Google Drive, iCloud, Dropbox)

REVIEW SHARED ACCOUNTS

- ☐ Phone plans – check account holder
- ☐ Streaming services (Netflix, Spotify, Disney+)
- ☐ Household utilities in joint names
- ☐ Insurance portals (car, home, health)

KEEP YOUR DIGITAL RECORDS SAFE

- ☐ Back up important documents (bank, payslips, property, school)
- ☐ Store copies in a secure folder or drive
- ☐ Email copies to your personal account (not shared)

PROTECT YOUR PRIVACY

- ☐ Check privacy settings on social media
- ☐ Consider who can view your accounts and make any necessary changes
- ☐ Turn off shared calendars or location sharing
- ☐ Sign out of old / shared devices

FOR PARENTS

- ☐ Set up a co-parenting app (Our Family Wizard, MyMob)
- ☐ Use neutral calendars for changeovers and school events
- ☐ Avoid using children's devices for communication with your former partner

Safety: If there are concerns about family violence or tech abuse, seek advice before making changes.

Family safety checklist

If you are ever in immediate danger, call Triple Zero.

This checklist is not exhaustive, but it may help you feel more prepared and supported.

IMMEDIATE SAFETY

- ☐ Save emergency numbers in your phone (Triple Zero, a trusted friend, local DV service).
- ☐ Identify a safe place you can go in an emergency (friend, family, refuge, police station).
- ☐ Pack a small 'go bag' with essentials (ID, bank card, keys, phone charger, medications).
- ☐ Teach your children how to call Triple Zero and practise a simple safety plan with them if appropriate.

HOME & PERSONAL SECURITY

- ☐ Change locks, security codes and garage remotes if safe to do so.
- ☐ Turn off or update any shared smart home devices (cameras, door locks, speakers).
- ☐ Review who has access to your car, house or spare keys.
- ☐ Keep a spare phone and some cash in a safe place if possible.

DIGITAL SAFETY

- ☐ Change passwords for email, banking and social media.
- ☐ Check location-sharing settings on phones, apps and devices.
- ☐ Log out of shared devices (computers, tablets, streaming services).
- ☐ Consider setting up a new email address just for sensitive communication.

LEGAL & SUPPORT

- ☐ Speak to a lawyer about protection orders or urgent parenting arrangements if needed.
- ☐ Contact 1800 RESPECT (1800 737 732) for 24/7 confidential advice and support.
- ☐ Ask your GP or a counsellor for referrals to support services.
- ☐ Record any incidents of violence or threats (dates, times, what happened).

LOOKING AHEAD

- ☐ Make a list of trusted people you can call on for help (family, friends, neighbours).
- ☐ Share your safety plan with one or two trusted people.
- ☐ If you move house, update your safety measures (locks, utilities, schools, mail redirection).

Important: Everyone's situation is different. Not all steps will be safe or appropriate for you – take only those that feel right and safe in your circumstances, and seek advice from professionals who understand family violence.

Your quick guide to Family Law lingo

Family Law has its own language, and it can feel overwhelming at first. This glossary is designed to give you plain-English explanations of the terms you're most likely to hear during separation and divorce.

AGREEMENTS & LEGAL DOCUMENTS

AGREEMENT

When you and your former partner reach a decision together about parenting or property arrangements. Can be informal (a handshake or notes) or formalised into a legally binding document.

BINDING FINANCIAL AGREEMENT (BFA)

A private contract about how property and finances will be divided. Each person must get independent legal advice for it to be valid.

CONSENT ORDERS

An agreement that's approved by the Court, making it legally binding and enforceable. Can cover both property and parenting matters.

PARENTING PLAN

A written agreement about care arrangements for children. Not legally binding but has legal effect.

FINAL ORDERS

The last Orders made by a Court (or by consent), setting out how parenting or property matters are to be resolved.

INTERIM ORDERS

Temporary Orders made by the Court until a final decision is reached.

PROCESSES & PATHWAYS

PATHWAY

The process you choose to resolve your separation – such as mediation, collaboration, negotiation or Court.

COLLABORATIVE PRACTICE

You, your former partner and both lawyers commit to working together respectfully (without going to Court) to resolve issues. Other professionals, like counsellors or financial experts, may also be involved.

MEDIATION

A process where you and your former partner meet with a neutral third person (the mediator) to try to reach an agreement. Mediators help with communication but do not make decisions for you.

FAMILY DISPUTE RESOLUTION (FDR)

A type of mediation required in most parenting cases before going to Court. Run by accredited mediators (FDR practitioners).

NEGOTIATION (THROUGH LAWYERS)

When your lawyer and your former partner's lawyer exchange proposals and work towards agreement on your behalf.

ROUND-TABLE CONFERENCE

A meeting where both parties and their lawyers sit down together to negotiate directly.

COURT PROCEEDINGS

When disputes are decided by a Judge. Usually the last resort if other options don't resolve matters.

PARENTING & FAMILY TERMS

BEST INTERESTS OF THE CHILD

The guiding principle for all parenting decisions – children's needs come first.

PARENTAL RESPONSIBILITY

The legal duties and powers parents have to make decisions for their children (e.g. health, education, religion).

CHANGEOVER

The handover of children from one parent to the other.

INDEPENDENT CHILDREN'S LAWYER (ICL)

A lawyer appointed by the Court to represent the best interests of a child. The ICL makes recommendations to the Court but does not take instructions directly from the child.

FAMILY VIOLENCE

Behaviour that controls, coerces or harms a family member. This can be physical, emotional, financial or psychological.

FINANCIAL & PROPERTY TERMS

PROPERTY POOL

The total of all assets (what you own) and liabilities (what you owe) that need to be divided after separation.

DISCLOSURE

The process of sharing important financial documents (such as bank statements, tax returns and super balances) so everyone negotiates with the same information. This is an ongoing duty, not a one-off.

VALUATION

Working out the market value of an asset, such as a house, car, business or superannuation.

EQUITY

The difference between the value of an asset and the debt owing on it. Example: if a house is worth $700,000 and the mortgage is $400,000, the equity is $300,000.

SUPERANNUATION SPLIT

An arrangement where part of one person's superannuation is transferred to the other as part of the settlement.

SPOUSAL MAINTENANCE

Payments from one former partner to the other to help meet reasonable living expenses when one person cannot adequately support themselves and the other has the capacity to pay.

OTHER COMMON LEGAL TERMS

DIVORCE

The legal end of a marriage. This is separate from parenting and property issues.

SEPARATION

When one or both people decide the relationship has ended. You don't need to be living in different houses to be considered separated.

SUBPOENA

A Court document requiring a person or organisation to provide documents or attend Court to give evidence.

WITHOUT PREJUDICE

A legal phrase meaning discussions or offers made in settlement negotiations can't later be used / shown to the Court if no agreement is reached.

Ready for your next step?

You've taken the time to read this book, reflect on your situation and start to understand the steps ahead. That's a big achievement. Now the most important thing you can do is get advice that's tailored to you and your family.

I would love the chance to help you work through this next chapter and for almost twenty years now I have owned and operated Brisbane Family Law Centre. And yes, our office hub is in Brisbane, but we have found ourselves helping families all across Australia. Our focus is always on helping you find the best way forward – whether that's through advice, negotiation or formalising your agreements.

At our partner service, Brisbane Family Mediation Centre, we help families have the important conversations needed to reach agreements without going to Court. Mediation can be held in person or online, and our experienced mediators provide a safe and structured process.

Not sure which service you need right now? Don't worry – just give my team a call. Whether you start with the law firm or the mediation centre, we'll guide you to the option that's best for you.

HOW TO REACH US

BRISBANE FAMILY LAW CENTRE

Phone: 07 3862 1955

Email: hello@bflc.com.au

Website: www.bflc.com.au

BRISBANE FAMILY MEDIATION CENTRE

Phone: 07 3613 6453

Email: mediation@brisbanefamilymediationcentre.com.au

Website: www.brisbanefamilymediationcentre.com.au

You don't have to figure this out on your own. We're here to listen, guide and support you through the next step – whatever that looks like for you.

www.ingramcontent.com/pod-product-compliance
Ingram Content Group UK Ltd.
Pitfield, Milton Keynes, MK11 3LW, UK
UKHW062008041026
15591UKWH00017B/1232

9 780994 202505